To Marilyn,
Best Wishes,
Karlene Hale

Copyright © 1995 Karlene K. Hale
Various articles reprinted with permission from the
Kennebec Journal, Augusta, Maine,
and the *Bangor Daily News*, Bangor, Maine.
All rights reserved. No part of this book may be
reproduced without permission in writing from the publisher.

Cover art by David Read.

ISBN 0-9639070-2-6

Published by

Dilligaf
PUBLISHING

64 Court Street, Ellsworth, Maine 04605

Being There

Profiles of Mental Illness

Karlene K. Hale

To My Elizabeth whose
Courage Inspired This Book

To My Husband John Who Became
A Believer

And to My Parents who Taught
Me The Value of Convictions

I Cannot Do

Going to school,
Away from home.
These are things that are hard.
But people have to grow up.
Working is
Something I cannot do.
Having a family is
Something I cannot do.
Having a drink is
Something I cannot do.
Going shopping is
Something I cannot do.
Mowing the lawn is
Something I cannot do.
Proving when I was first mentally ill is
Something I cannot do.

Table of Contents

Introduction xii

Foreward: What is Mental Illness? xvii

We're Human Beings, Too 1

I Take My Meds and I Do My Best 7

I'll Do Anything for a Cigarette 12

I Didn't Know What To Do 16

He Was Going To Be Our College Grad 23

What Did We Get For $18 Million? 29

I Felt Like a Circus Freak 36

She Was Quite a Lady 48

It Was Pure Fright. I Became So Scared 55

Would You Feel This Way About My Son If He Had Cancer? ... 60

I Thought the Hospital Was the White House 65

I Can't Get Mad, I Can't Have a Good Cry 72

The Only Thing I Had Was Being Down and Out 78

Our Daughter's Illness Is Everything 83

Some People Have No Sympathy 90

I Missed Everything 97

Introduction

This book really began more than five years ago, when my only child, Elizabeth Washburn, was diagnosed as manic depressive at the age of sixteen. She probably had been sick for some years before that, but my husband and I attributed her spectacular temper tantrums, her spending sprees, her midnight walks, her weeping spells, and her flights of fancy to a difficult adolescence.

As a young child, she was beautiful, insightful, sensitive, highly intelligent, and very social. By seventh grade, there was moodiness, increasing absenteeism from school, projects that were started but never finished, and a general sense of unhappiness.

She told me she was hearing voices; I didn't take it seriously enough.

She lost friends at school, friends who suddenly decided she was not cool enough for their inner circle. Losing her best friend was the largest wound of all.

We took her to a counselor in eighth grade, and again during her sophomore year. He called me at work one day and said Elizabeth did not need counseling, that it was a luxury for her. He had young people who really needed his help, he said.

In high school, Elizabeth was brilliant in speech and drama. She had the lead in the school play as a sophomore, then laid on the couch and refused to go to school for nearly a month after the play ended.

The illness became full-blown during her sophomore year in high school, when we finally took her out of school in March and ordered lessons through a correspondence school.

Every morning became a struggle to get her out of bed. Some days I was successful, other days, I was not. Her main problem was insomnia. She often could not fall asleep until dawn, and would spend the hours before that tossing with anxiety. Sometimes she left the house for walks, and I would get up in the middle of the night to find her gone.

She also was terribly in love with her first boyfriend, who shared that love. The two of them would meet at night and talk, or maybe fall asleep in a lilac garden about a mile from our house.

Her summers were spent going to theater workshops or to other programs designed to enhance her dramatic talent.

Things went down hill immediately at the beginning of her junior year in high school. By October, we were told she would receive no academic credit for that year because she had already used up all her absences by the fourth week of the school year.

In the meantime, she shaved her head, became so headstrong that we were almost afraid of her, and fell in with a boy who ultimately proved to be a very poor influence.

The school, meanwhile, treated her as a rebel, rather than a student who might have psychiatric problems. Each thing she loved was taken away from her in some way by her school. At one point, she had a small photography exhibit at the school. When she went to collect her pictures, they had been taken out of the case and stepped on, leaving them dirty and spoiled. When Elizabeth complained to the principal, he said, "Well, what would you expect, Elizabeth?"

She was taunted in the cafeteria, hounded constantly by teachers for back homework, and had few friends. All the while, without our knowing it, she was sinking deeper and deeper into mental illness.

The last straw came when the principal at her school pulled her out of the regional gifted and talented program, because she was behind on her school work.

That evening, she seemed disoriented, distant, somewhat incoherent. I said she could stay home and rest until she healed from all her setbacks.

It was a suicide note left on my coffee table in the middle of the night that brought us to the point of seeking professional help again. Elizabeth's friend wrote the note, saying he was very worried, that she wasn't making any sense, that she was talking of taking her own life.

Within hours we were in the office of a psychologist in Lewiston. A few weeks later, we were hooked up to one of the best child and adolescent psychiatrists in Maine.

Elizabeth was dressed for the appointment all in black, with eyes accented by black eyeliner, hair dyed black and spiked, and too much mascara. I expected the doctor to do a double take when he saw her. He did not.

"Come in, please," he said, ushering us into an office furnished like a comfortable living room. We were all silent for several seconds.

"So, what's been going on?" he finally asked casually.

Like many parents of mentally ill children, I thought Elizabeth would be put on a course of lithium and everything would be fine. She would return to her old self and life would continue as always.

For a lucky few, that is the case. But lithium is effective only sixty-six percent of the time. Usually other medications are needed to boost the effect.

Going to see the psychiatrist was only the beginning, not the end. Elizabeth and I knew there were two ways we could go with her illness: deny it, or learn all we could about it. We chose the latter.

For more than two years, I left work early every Tuesday to take Elizabeth to the psychologist for talking therapy. It was a three-hour chunk out of the day by the time we got to the appointment, sat through the hour, then returned home. Sometimes, we made the trip twice if she had to see the psychiatrist in the same week, as she did at first. All this was carried out while I held down a full-time newspaper job.

My husband rarely took her to the appointments. He also is a reporter, at the Maine State House, and he never seemed to be able to leave his job. The implication was that his work was more important than mine, something I resented. I learned that mental illness is primarily a feminist issue, with mothers doing most of the caring.

Elizabeth was put on a variety of medications, to see what might work. And because they were so expensive, I could not fill a whole prescription at once; so I stopped at the drugstore on the way home at least once a week, usually every two or three days, for refills. Her medications were taking most of my paycheck, and I had to pay up front for them before the insurance reimbursement a month or so later.

While all this was going on, we transferred Elizabeth to another school outside our own town. We took out a home equity loan to pay the tuition. It was one of the smartest things we ever did.

She thrived at the new school, where she made friends, and the school staff understood her illness. She was given a tutor when she had to miss school because of depression, and her mood swings were accommodated. There were days when staying at school was too much, and someone would bring her home, or I would be called at work to come get her.

The stress was enormous for our family, but at least we were working toward something, not groping in the dark, mystified.

She was hospitalized only once for any length of time, about ten days at St. Mary's Regional Hospital in Lewiston for depression.

But there were incidents of loss of impulse control. She knicked her wrists, took behavioral risks, smashed out windows, and at one point, two weeks after starting college in New York City, took too many Klonipin, a tranquilizer. The school refused to allow her to stay in the dorm anymore, and my husband and I had to make an emergency trip to New York to find housing and release her from the hospital. She eventually became too ill to continue with the school.

She is now twenty-one, doing quite well and living in Boston. She has not given up her dream of becoming an actress and her health seems to become better each year. Plus, we know help is always available.

Because of this one courageous girl, I developed an interest in all mental illness. I learned that most people with these diseases become impoverished, that they lack adequate housing, and are shunned and discriminated against by society.

The mentally ill daily feel the piercing eye of scorn for something they cannot help, or they feel the condescending hand of pity.

Yet there are triumphs in the face of adversity, dramatic stories of recovery and of fighting back against a system that often fails its most vulnerable citizens.

This book tells some of those stories, through the words and eyes of the mentally ill and family members. To all who participated, I am deeply grateful and sympathetic.

Karlene K. Hale

FOREWARD

What is Mental Illness?

Major mental illness can be divided into two categories. Thought disorder and mood disorders.

Thought disorders include schizophrenia and related illnesses, while mood disorders cover major depression and bipolar disease, or manic depression, as it is more commonly known.

Both illnesses are now considered to be biological, caused by chemical imbalances in the brain. While there are many theories about why the imbalances ocur, the most popular theory is that they are genetic, then triggered by a major stressful life event, such as a loss or a traumatic experience. Most mental illness begins between the ages of eighteen and twenty-four, at the time of life when the young person leaves for college or takes a first job.

Other doctors believe the illnesses are caused by a virus contracted by the mother during pregnancy or by the patient early in life. The virus lies dormant for years before erupting during a period of stress, these doctors theorize.

The environment plays a role by causing the stress that sends people prone to mental illness into episodes. Most people with mental disorders, even when they are fully recovered, tend to have low stress levels. They cannot take as much stimulation as those without such diseases.

We do know one thing. Mental illness is not caused by bad parenting, as was thought for years, or by growing up in poverty and squalor. Scientists know that the socio-economic theory of mental illness, popular in the 1960's, is wrong, because conditions in the nation's cities are becoming worse, yet the rate of mental illness, especially schizophrenia, which was once thought to be social in origin, is not on the rise.

The symptoms of schizophrenia and other thought disorders include a diminished ability to think clearly and logically; delusions, including the belief that others are plotting against you or that you are a religious person given special powers; seeing or hearing things, especially voices warning of danger or telling you what to do; and apathy, agitation, anxiety, social withdrawal, and lack of emotional expression.

Hospitalization is usually required for severe schizophrenia, often for the safety of the ill person. Hospitalization also offers a chance to try medication and monitor how it works.

Common medications, all anti-psychotic drugs, given for schizophrenia, are Prolixin, Haldol, Navane, Stelazine, Loxitane, Daxolin, Mellaril, Thorazine, Clozoril, and Risperdone.

Mood disorders sometimes are called "affective" disorders, and encompass manic depression and major depressive upset.

The symptoms of depression are abnormal sadness, feelings of helplessness, extreme fatigue or insomnia, anxiety, lack of interest in surroundings, sometimes hostility, and thoughts of suicide.

Mania is exhibited by extreme excitement, constant talking, spending sprees and other excessive behavior, unusually high energy level, ability to get by on little sleep, and enhanced feelings of well-being or grandiosity.

The most common cycle of symptoms in manic depression and major depression are changes in sleep patterns, and in energy and activity level, changes in appetite, mood, self-esteem, thinking, speech, sex drive, and personal relationships.

Medications given for mood disorders are lithium, Norpramin, Trofranil, Aventyl, Pamelor, Elavil, Trazodone, Prozac, Zoloft, and Ludiomil.

It often takes a number of trials with different medications to find the combination that best suits the patient. Someone with bipolar disease, for example, usually needs a mood stabilizer, such as Lithium, plus an antidepressant, and sometimes, a tranquilizer.

Thought disorders require anti-psychotic drugs to calm the hallucinations, plus a tranquilizer or antidepressant to quell the secondary symptoms, such as lack of motivation.

The above information is contained in literature from the Alliance for the Mentally Ill of Maine and is available from the National Alliance for the Mentally Ill.

We're Human Beings Too

The boy who once ran the basketball freely up the court now sits all day by the window, staring at nothing.

Projects lie unfinished, meals untouched.

Friends call, then gradually drift away. And one by one all the stars go out as the sharp shadow of mental illness descends, piercing the brain in a million places.

Mark LaValle knows the agony of a mind gone haywire. "It is hard. It is so hard to admit you have an illness that even you can't understand," LaValle, forty-three, said. "It robs you. Mental illness robs you of your whole life."

He has been diagnosed at least six times, each time receiving a different opinion, from schizophrenia to neurosis with depression. Now after years of different diagnoses and doctors, LaValle just refers to his illness as a personality disorder.

He spends much of his time at the LINC social club in Augusta, where he helps other members regain the living skills they either lost to illness or never had the time to develop before the hammer struck.

"You're fighting stigma and the emotional pain of losing control. You're fighting an illness that takes away the chance to improve your life," he said of the brutal impact.

People with mental illness lose friends, while insurance and family savings are ground into tiny shreds as the disease takes its toll. Life becomes so upside down that only the Furies reign.

"It isn't a disease I would wish on anyone," said Grace M. who did not want her last name used because of lingering shame that dogs people with mental illness.

LaValle and Grace M. are among an estimated two hundred eighty adults in the greater Augusta area who suffer from chronic and severe mental illness and depend upon the community for services.

That number is at least twice as many as would be expected for Augusta and surrounding towns statistically. The area population is about thirty-six thousand. The figure also does not include mentally ill persons who are under private insurance, primarily children and adolescents. Most adults lost their insurance long ago.

Assuming that three percent of the population suffers from severe mental illness, one would expect about one hundred eight people in the state capitol to be afflicted.

The Augusta Mental Health Institute, however, is a huge magnet that has drawn the mentally ill to the city. Upon release from AMHI, as many as thirty-eight percent of the former patients stay in the area, to be near the hospital and mental health services.

That means Kennebec County, with ten percent of the state's population of 1.1 million, is home to more than one-third of those coming out of the state hospital.

At the same time, three to five people a month move from other parts of the state to Augusta, to be near the hospital and ancillary services.

And with the average length of stay at Augusta Mental Health Institute becoming shorter and shorter, from a period of months to only a few weeks, as many as thirty patients a month are coming back into the community from the hospital. That figure includes repeat admissions who nevertheless have to be integrated into the community all over again.

The result is a looming crisis in care as more and more former patients press harder and harder on community resources that already are too thinly stretched.

People who have chronic mental illness need housing, job training, outpatient therapy, medication, places to socialize. They also need help getting through the maze of forms and paperwork for disability benefits, food stamps, and other programs.

While most originally came from middle or upper middle-class families, the mentally ill in the state system are impoverished; their energy, money and earning power sapped by years of the powerfully devastating sickness.

"It's hard getting through the system," said Kenneth Jauron, executive director of the Bread of Life Ministries which runs a soup kitchen and shelter.

About half the one hundred forty people who eat at the kitchen each day have mental illness, and the ten-bed shelter, when full, usually has five people with mental illness who are scraping along the edge of the system.

Stretched community resources and cutbacks in state funding for all social programs, including mental health, are leaving some in unsuitable housing or no housing at all.

Home is sometimes a room that can fit only one person, a room with one light hanging from the ceiling, cracks in the walls, a cot, and a bathroom down the hall.

"Some just go from place to place, staying with friends," Jauron said. "The services are not keeping up with the discharge rate at Augusta Mental Health Institute."

But the need for services differs.

Mark has been hospitalized only once, for three days. He has his own apartment, is engaged to be married, and is using his Social Security benefits "to get my life together," he said.

He is on a plan devised by Social Security to get new eyeglasses, a driver's license, and training to become a worker in the mental health field.

Yet because he is on Medicaid he had difficulty finding a dentist to fix his abscessed teeth, and he wound up going to the emergency room at Kennebec Valley Medical Center, for penicillin. Hospital emergency rooms often become the doctor's office for the mentally ill.

When the teeth bothered him more than ever a day later and he developed a fever, he went back to the hospital, walking the distance in a rain storm.

Grace has been hospitalized thirty times at Augusta Mental Health Institute since she was eighteen years old; she is now forty. In between the stretches at the state hospital that lasted anywhere from two years to two months, there were brief stays at other, private hospitals.

Her last hospitalization was in 1991.

"I've been in the mental health system for twenty-three years," she said. Grace, diagnosed as manic depressive, doesn't talk very much. Her hands tremble and when she speaks, she picks at her fingernails.

She has lived in group homes and now has her own apartment on the city's east side. It is the first time in nine years that she has lived on her own.

She also is working six hours a week as a clerk in a local store, her way of getting back into a job market that left her behind because of repeated hospitalization. She will go back into the workplace gradually.

She began by working only fifteen minutes, then a half-hour, then working up to more time, as her stress level allowed.

Grace became sick when she was in nurse's training in Lewiston. "I just went into an illness I couldn't get out of," she said. In those early years, she would return to her parents' home in Wiscasset after being released from the hospital. She had a therapist but little else in the way of aftercare or support.

Community services are much better now than fifteen or twenty years ago, she said. She now has a therapist, takes medication that fits her disorder more accurately, receives help from a mental health worker, and has friends at the social club.

Yet she worries about money, as do most mentally ill. She lives on four hundred fifty dollars a month in disability, plus the small amount she makes from her job. She receives food stamps and Medicaid. Her rent is two hundred dollars a month. Some former patients pay as much as seventy-five percent of their disability checks on rent.

There is little left over for Grace; a shopping spree is a trip to Goodwill Industries. There is little beauty in her life.

"I go out for supper with a friend once in a while," she said. While hospitalizations and poverty are tough, slurs from society hurt more, she and Mark said.

People with mental illness are more likely to be harrassed and tormented than other people, because they sometimes dress strangely or talk to voices only they can hear. They are simply more vulnerable, perceived as weaker and more easily fooled, Mark said.

"The hardest thing through all the years has been the stigma, the ignorance, the lack of understanding," Grace said.

Mark put it this way, "We're human beings too; we deserve our place in the sun."

Donald Robbins remembers spending about four months out of every year at the psychiatric unit at the Veteran Hospital at Togus. The voices he hears all the time would become unbearable and Robbins, thirty-seven, would check into the hospital, where he would be put on a combination of drugs and therapy.

The drugs, he said, "keep away the big guys," the cacophony of sounds that in the past have taken the form of the Lord of Truth, the Lord of Life, and the Lord of Earth.

Donald has schizophrenia.

He and ninety-nine other patients who twenty years ago would have lived at Togus are now in a day treatment program that gives them therapy and support during the day, while allowing them to return home at night.

The day program is a half-step between the hospital and the community. It is for people who need more support than the community can give, but less than required at the hospital.

Kennebec Valley Medical Center has a similar program for nonveterans who do not need the twenty-four hour services of a hospital.

"What is the best utilization of resources? To warehouse or to offer a diverse day program?" asked Marianne MacDonald, director of the Togus program.

Donald comes to the hospital five days a week in the Togus van. He delivers medical records throughout the hospital, a job that pays two hundred dollars a month. That, coupled with a disability check, gives him seven hundred eight-five dollars a month to live on. The day program provides structure and direction, giving patients a chance to re-learn skills lost to mental illness.

Togus treats about five thousand veterans a year for psychiatric disorders, ranging from severe mental illness to Post Traumatic Stress Disorder. About eighty percent of the five thousand are repeat patients.

The hospital also contracts with the Department of Veterans Affairs to run a network of boarding homes in the area. Other patients live in "rent a room places," one of the doctors said.

"A high percentage of people do not have strong family support," said Dr. Clifford Davis, director of the acute inpatient psychiatric unit. The day program tries to give the support that otherwise would be given by families.

"We deal with the here and now and how to make life better," MacDonald said. There is no arguing with patients about whether delusions are real and no time wasted on discussing what symptoms mean.

"The emphasis is on the quality of life, with vets helping vets," she said. "Our whole goal is to keep people out of the hospital."

Robbins has not been hospitalized for three years; there is no time limit on how long he can stay in the day program.

He was twenty-three when the voices began, after he grew up in a large neighborhood in Gardiner, played sports in high school, served in the Marine Corps, went to computer school, and took a job with Data General in Massachusetts.

"It started with one voice, a girl's voice," he said, "then there were more and more and more. I walked miles and miles listening to voices," he said.

He quit his job because he thought employees were talking about him and conspiring against him. When the voices of the employees continued, he would walk into the plant and tell the workers to stop it.

Friends suggested he go into a hospital in Massachusetts, and, after a few months of treatment, the voices went away. Donald re-enlisted in the military and the voices came back, this time sounding like his aging or dead relatives. He obtained a medical discharge from the service and began twelve years of hospitalization.

He lived for awhile at a VA boarding home, but now has his own room in Gardiner. Evenings he walks around town, sometimes stopping for a meal.

"Before I came here, I thought I was the only person who had this," he said of his illness. Now he knows there are others, that he is not alone.

He is aiming for a job outside the hospital, and he will probably make it, MacDonald said. But she knows the limits of her program and the limitations of the patients. "Some of them will probably be here until they die," she said.

I Take My Meds and I Do My Best

Mark Tibbetts once slashed his wrist in front of a psychiatrist in a dramatic attempt to get some help.

The most that doctors seemed able to tell him was that he had an adjustment disorder, one that was not helped much by his big-time use of cocaine.

Tibbetts, now thirty-four, was a wheeler-dealer, shooting up two thousand dollars worth of cocaine a week at the height of his drug habit and using workers' compensation checks to invest in an acquaintance's drug business.

"I made a lot of money," he said.

He also became sicker and sicker as his already troubled mind short-circuited over and over, throwing him into the hospital again and again.

There were stays at the Augusta Mental Health Institute, at Kennebec Valley Medical Center in Augusta, at St. Mary's Regional Hospital in Lewiston, and at Seton Unit at Mid-Maine Medical in Waterville.

It was at St. Mary's that he went through a drug rehabilitation program that marked the first step in staying clean.

But eight years ago, with lightning still surging through his brain, Mark wound up at Seton, where he finally received the correct diagnosis for his illness: Manic Depression.

The diagnosis fit exactly his mood pattern of excitement and grandiose plans followed eventually by periods of hopelessness and despair.

"I never felt quite OK mentally," he said. Mark grew up in southern Maine, and even as a child, he had a low stress level and an exaggerated sensitivity to even the smallest slights.

"If I had an argument with a friend, I would be devastated," he said. That is a common feature of manic depression, to internalize every detail of one's life, to become obsessive about whose fault the quarrel was, what can be done to rectify things.

The private hospitals, meanwhile, offered the adult Mark the structure required to put in order a life out of control. In the private settings, there were daily visits from the doctor, group therapy, one-on-one therapy with staff, and a regular time for meals and medications.

The state hospital was seen as a place to crash for awhile, a place where nothing was required of him, Mark said. "You're not made to do anything there," he said, adding that services are offered, but whether patients take advantage of them is another issue.

"If you stay out of the staff's way, don't flip out, or cause a danger to yourself or others, you can float right through there," he said.

It was less easy to stay afloat in the community once he was released.

There he encountered a fractured system of services that is feeling the strain of overload as more and more patients come out of Augusta Mental Health Institute and state funding needed to run community programs fails to keep pace.

"I had no place to live. I had two sets of clothes," Mark said. He moved into the Bread of Life homeless shelter in Augusta and lived on workers' compensation checks. He later picked up some clothes at the Augusta Mental Health Institute thrift shop and moved into a tiny room. "I call it just existing. I had no idea how to get entitlements. I had to get a lawyer to help me get disability checks."

Mark's experience is not unusual.

The whole problem is that while services have increased within the community, the number of patients being released has increased even more rapidly, said Linwood Diket, Augusta Mental Health Institute's aftercare coordinator for central Maine.

The hospital is supposed to provide an individual support plan for each patient being released, including needs for housing, aftercare, counseling, and job training, if necessary.

Those plans, however, often go awry, Diket said. "The biggest problem is that the patients are unwilling to trust a system that they see as unresponsive," he said.

He also acknowledged that there is a lack of aggressive follow-up once patients leave the hospital, due to sheer numbers. When Diket began working at Augusta Mental Health Institute in 1971, the hospital had about seventeen hundred patients, many of whom were expected to spend their lives there.

With the breakthrough in medications and new laws that decree that patients must be in the least restrictive environment, the number of admissions is down to about twenty a month, while thirty or more patients leave the hospital each month. Many are repeat patients.

"Augusta Mental Health Institute is the last stop on the psychiatric trail," Diket said. "It is the most restrictive and most stays are involuntary." The average length of stay is now twenty-three days or less.

The director of Kennebec Valley Mental Health Center, John Shaw, is more blunt. He is convinced the whole system of state support for the mentally ill is in chaos, in crisis.

"Services for adults are inadequate, and for children, even more inadequate," he said.

The mental health center in Augusta already has more patients than it can accommodate and there is a waiting list, he said. Patients who complain of "assembly-line therapy," whereby they see a doctor for fifteen minutes each month, are not making baseless complaints, Shaw said.

The center provides emergency therapy, emergency care and medication, and help in locating community services. In any given year, about one thousand three hundred seventy adults and children pass through the doors of the center, some only once, some every week.

Shaw said the future holds more strain for already over-whelmed services, while greater numbers of people, like Mark, will be under-served or not served at all.

So the transition from hospital to community is not the effortless one envisioned by those drawn up hospital release plans.

There is one agency in central Maine that helps adults with mental illness find housing and jobs. It is Motivational Services, Corp., founded in 1976 when the explosion of drugs found to helpful in treating mental disease emptied out the state hospital.

Motivational Services helps at least two hundred eighty people with mental disease make their way back into the community. The agency, funded by federal, state and local money, also runs a social club and offers assistance in filling out the endless stream of forms required for public assistance.

Richard Weiss, executive director of the agency, is a soft-spoken psychologist with a goatee and a direct gaze. He points with some pain to the number of obstacles encountered by the mentally ill as they join the community.

"There is not an adequate amount of affordable housing," he said. The majority of people with mental illness receive about four hundred twenty-four dollars a month in supplemental insurance or disability benefits.

"They're impoverished. They're always living on the edge," Weiss said. "There is the constant stress of getting by."

No more than thirty percent of benefits should be going for rent, he said, but some former patients pay as much as seventy percent of their income for housing. The housing often is one room in an inferior neighborhood.

There also is the need for clothes, transportation and medical services; and it is important that housing be within walking distance of medical facilities or a job program, because most former patients do not have cars. Some never learned to drive.

Weiss said such things as taking medications on time or keeping appointments with therapists cannot be addressed until the basic necessities of life are met. "They need to know that things will be predictable, that they will know where they will live, where their next meal is coming from."

His organization runs three supervised homes in Augusta, each offering twenty-four hour supervision for up to nine people. When the former patients are able, they move into their apartments or take a room. The average stay at the supervised homes is two years.

"Some are nice, some are not so nice," is the way Weiss described the lodgings the patients find.

Larry Fleury, owner of River City Realty, is the controversial owner of about twenty rooms and apartments that he rents to the mentally ill. He also provides shelter for other low-income tenants.

Most of the apartment fires within the city occur at one of Fleury's places, while others accuse him of bilking the mentally ill for substandard housing. Fleury said he is offering a service that no one else in the city will offer.

"We treat them all on an individual basis," he said of his tenants. "Some work out well, some not so well." He has not had to evict a tenant for years, mainly because he calls family members or social workers to act as go-betweens if there is rowdiness or anti-social behavior.

"On a grass roots level, the state system is doing a much better job now in keeping track of the mentally ill than ten years ago," he said.

"This is a much easier time to be working with the mentally ill."

Housing may be the biggest problem facing a newly released patient, but employment is just as important in the long run.

That is because mental illness usually strikes young people between the ages of eighteen and twenty-four, just as they are getting their feet wet in the world of work. The strain of the illness obliterates any job skills the young people may have had.

"Intellectually, they can compete," Weiss said. "Emotionally they can't" in the aftermath of interrupted lives. Some have previously failed in the workplace and are terrified of going back.

Fifty-nine people who use Motivational Services are employed, a number Weiss considers high. But all jobs are entry-level, with an hourly wage of anywhere from four dollars and twenty-five cents to seven dollars.

"It is our objective to motivate people, to keep them going, even when they have failed," Weiss said.

The real aim of Motivational Services is to offer support to a population most in need of it. "These people are at the risk of being homeless, they lack training or education, and they lack support and skills. Hospitals and mental health centers have a role, but the greatest need is everyday coping skills and supports," Weiss said.

Mark, who has two years of divinity school, did not turn to Motivational Services, because he did not think he needed what it offered.

But he keeps structure in his life.

"Each day there must be something to accomplish," he said. He has joined the Board of Directors of Bread of Life Ministries and wants a constructive place in society again.

"I'm no different from someone with diabetes, man. I take my meds and I do my best."

I'll do Anything for a Cigarette

Inside the filthy little room, jammed to the walls by a twin-sized bed, television, a compact refrigerator and strewn bits of garbage, Stephen Ferris stood shivering as he spoke with the policeman.

"You feeling good?" asked patrolman Robert Gregoire who was forced to stand in the hallway because the room is too small for two men to sit.

"Fair," Ferris answered. His pale skinny frame, clad only in stained brown corduroy pants and a threadbare T-shirt quaked as though in seizure.

"You cold?" the policeman asked, looking to the mattress, stained dark gray and without sheets, then to the grimy, hole-ridden blanket atop it.

"With these blankets, it's hard to stay warm," Ferris said, also looking to the blanket. It is November, when temperatures in Maine can go below freezing at night.

"That's not your medication making you shiver like that?" Gregoire asked. "You're taking your medications, right?"

Ferris, who came to Augusta seven years ago after living in Portland, assured the officer he was taking the pills.

Their conversation completed, the officer left.

There are hundreds of people with mental illness in the Augusta area who are capable of caring for themselves. City police, however, deal daily with people like Stephen who either refuse help or cannot use the routine kind of services offered within the community.

The result is a group of people, Stephen among them, who have been discharged from hospitals, but are not capable of living on their own. They often behave in ways that threaten the well-being of others or their own safety. Some have substance abuse problems along with mental illness, others refuse to take their medications. All are falling through the cracks of the social services safety net.

Police are called only when a person's behavior becomes a nuisance or a danger. One woman cuts herself, more than one hundred times in the past few years. A man drives around the city in an old pickup truck loaded with rotting garbage. A third person reacts violently when children taunt him about his strange looks.

Involuntary committals to the hospital are a time-consuming, careful procedure that must be followed to the letter. And police or facility members can go through all the initial steps, only to have the mentally ill person turned away on the doorstep of the state mental hospital. Hospitals now will take only those who present a clear and immediate danger to themselves or others. A mental crisis or simply weird behavior is not enough.

The commital process is one that provides lots of space for diverting the person to a less restrictive environment than a hospital.

The committall process begins when the person harms himself or others or threatens to. Family members or a landlord often make the first call to police.

A law enforcement agent must then determine that the person is dangerous. An evaluation must be done at a local general hospital emergency room or health center. If the clinician on duty decides the person is dangerous or mentally ill, a licensed psychiatrist is called in to make a determination. If that doctor agrees, then the person can be hospitalized upon a judge's order.

If the person is very violent, he or she can be taken directly to the state hospital without going through the other steps.

The procedure is designed to protect patients' rights while at the same time, preventing an overloading of beds reserved for involuntary admissions.

Patients sometimes are placed in a social services out-patient program instead of being hospitalized. Or they voluntarily go to a private hospital that offers psychiatric care.

Involuntary committal to the state hospital is considered the last resort. Once the patient arrives at the hospital, he or she is interviewed again, by a staff doctor who decides if the hospital will accept the person.

In 1992-1993, the Augusta Mental Health Institute took in six hundred involuntary admissions, and in 1993-1994, more than eight hundred. Many are repeat patients. The hospital was so flooded that it tightened its standards, leaving the private hospitals to fill the void by taking some short-term committals.

But only the state's largest hospitals have beds for psychiatric patients, and not many beds at that, no more than sixteen in most hospitals. Others have only a handful, four or five.

A patient can be held involuntarily at Augusta Mental Health Institute for up to five days. If staff believe the person should stay longer, the District Court must be petitioned. The patient then must receive two evaluations by separate doctors. If both agree that the patient is still dangerous, the judge can order a committal for up to four months the first time, and up to a year on subsequent stays.

Most involuntary patients are released from Augusta Mental Health Institute within two weeks, others stay voluntarily, and about one hundred and fifty a year receive a court committal. Again, some of the patients are repeats.

A patient can refuse medication and other treatment at the hospital, even if put there involuntarily.

Stephen said he has been committed "quite a few times," for periods ranging from one month to as long as nine months.

He also spent a year at the Pineland Center for the Retarded in Pownal, because he sniffed gasoline, he said.

Stephen claims his brother dropped him on his head when he was a boy, which led to his mental illness. He does not keep written records doctors or others give him, so he is unsure of his official diagnosis.

Mostly he gets into trouble with the police for harming himself or threatening or harming other people. But he only gets into trouble when he runs out of cigarettes, he is quick to add.

"I fight real bad and dirty, so I have to have a cigarette right away to calm down," he said. "They make me feel all right. They make me feel steady. I'll do anything for a cigarette."

Most mentally ill people police encounter simply refuse to take any help, others do not have the mental capacity to use the available services.

"The majority of them just don't like mental health agencies," said Augusta Sgt. Peter Couture. "Number one, they don't feel they are getting the help they need, and number two, a lot of them are tired of just getting pills."

Stephen said he does not like to take medications a man brings to him every week, except for the sleeping pills. Stephen gives the other drugs away.

"I've only had a doctor force medications on me once. And I drew off and punched him one."

Augusta Mental Health Institute, he said, offers good food, and the staff treats him well and makes sure he budgets his money while he is there. He also can watch television and talk with a lot of people.

But Stephen said he is trying to become "less involved" with AMHI, mostly because the hospital restricts his smoking and will not let him leave when he wants to.

His love of cigarettes is obvious within his apartment. Butts are ground out everywhere, on the television stand, on the refrigerator, on the floor.

Workers from one social service agency are trying to teach Stephen how to cook, and he does not mind their periodic visits.

But the social workers can sometimes be pushy about telling him what to do, and he does not like that, he said. Although he sees his family from time to time, he does not like to talk about them and does not want their help.

Living conditions are not considered part of the danger equation for people with mental illness. As a result, many of them do not eat for days on end, and live in tiny rooming-house hovels infested with roaches.

Abusive neighbors often steal drugs, money, or anything else of value from vulnerable people like Stephen. The mentally ill person sometimes sees this kind of behavior as an expression of friendship.

"They are put in these places among the alcoholics, the druggies, the criminal element," Coutoure said. "It's almost like the mentally ill are seeing this, and they think that's the way they have to live."

Stephen said his neighbors, many of whom have mental illness, substance abuse, or criminal records, do not steal from him or treat him badly. "I told them, as long as they don't take anything from me, I'll help them. They treat me pretty well."

Stephen said social workers have told him the condition of his apartment is a disgrace, a health problem. But he disagrees. The germs do not bother him, he said, because he is around them all the time and has built up immunities.

In fact, Stephen said he is more than happy with the way he lives and sees nothing wrong with it, regardless of what others say.

"I've gotten very used to it. It's my decision."

I Didn't Know What to Do

The first picture shows a chubby-cheeked baby napping in his crib, his face a study in peace. In the second photograph is a young boy in a football uniform striking a pose. The third depicts a middle-age man with a beard and longish hair.

That last picture was taken of Scott King during his family's last happy Christmas. In December of 1993, right on the verge of the holiday, King took his own life by hanging himself from a tree after years of anguish and despair of mental illness ate at his brain.

His mother, Ruth, still weeps when she talks about the tragedy and the years leading up to it.

His father, Frederick, a former wilderness guide who feels guilt because he was too strict with his son, does not weep. He makes wry jokes and bitter comments.

"He did a good job of it. He broke his neck and died instantly. I guess he didn't want his old man criticizing him for his last act," Frederick said of his son's death. Then he looks out the window and is silent.

Ruth is eighty-eight years old and to look at her, one would think she could be twenty years younger. She has a serenity about her face that others might envy. What she has gone through is not readily apparent.

But when she begins to talk, the pain is there, and the guilt. "Frederick and I were not very good parents. Fred was very hard on Scott, and I was insecure. Scott always wanted his father's praise, but he did not get it very often, so I tried to make it up to him."

Scott was the oldest of three children, and was born when his mother was in her late thirties. "We just hoped so hard for a boy, we didn't even have any girl names picked out."

She later had two more children, both girls, when she was approaching her early forties.

The Kings were probably fine parents and are blaming themselves needlessly. Mental illness is not caused by bad parenting, experts now agree. We now know that such illnesses are the result of chemical imbalances in the brain, imbalances that Scott might have been born with.

"Scott told me several times while he was growing up that he didn't feel like he fit in, and I guess he never did," his mother said. He was an average student, one who baffled guidance counselors who said he was very bright and should be doing better in school. "They said he lacked motiviation," his mother said. "But Scott was not lazy."

As he went through school, there were some behavioral problems, but nothing that pointed to any severe problems. He played football, basketball and baseball, and was in Cony High School's famous annual variety show, Chizzle Wizzle. He was popular, but he did not think he was.

Ruth tried to say tactfully that Scott could have been friendly with boys and girls from the nicest families in Augusta.

"But he always chose a different kind of friend, boys from backgrounds not like his," she said.

Scott graduated from Cony in 1961 and went to the University of Maine in Orono. "He came home almost every weekend. Now that's not healthy for a college student, I don't think."

In his final year of school, he discovered a love of mathematics and his grades soared. He graduated in 1965 and went to teach in Searsport.

"Oh, my, he was scared. He had such pains in his stomach that he woke up the landlady where he was rooming and she called a doctor. It was nerves, just nerves," Ruth continued.

A year later, he married, went to Louisiana to earn his master's degree, and almost immediately began having marital problems.

"His wife called two months after they were married and said they were getting a divorce," Ruth said. "Scott was becoming difficult to live with."

The couple stayed together for a few more years, Scott spent some time in the U.S. Navy, then took a job with a corporation in Connecticut.

"Frederick gets up very early, and one morning at five a.m., he looked out the window and said, "Scott is here, and he's driving a motorcycle.' He had given up the job in Hartford and had simply come home," his mother said.

Shortly after, he burned all his high school yearbooks, all his yearbooks from college, even a scrapbook of his growing up years that his mother compiled one year for him. "Oh, how much those things would mean to me now."

He took a teaching job in Livermore Falls, and his mother has every reason to believe he was an excellent teacher. "He had the ability to make people feel worthwhile. And he was unconventional and drove a motorcycle. The students, from all I've heard, loved him. He felt the textbooks were not appropriate for students from a mill town, so he adjusted his math problems to their real lives. He'd say things like, "You have a motorcycle and it costs so much..." she said.

But Ruth also believes Scott did not belong in the classroom for the last two or three years he was teaching. He was heavily into alcohol and drugs and his life was becoming out of control. He had married a woman he dated for seven years and the marriage did not last any time.

"She used to call me and say, 'Ruth, do you ever hear Scott say very, very strange things?"

Scott resigned from his teaching job very abruptly. He went to the principal's office, said he wanted to quit and that he wanted to leave that day. The school let him go, which made his mother think they were glad to get rid of him. "I really think the only reason they kept him as long as they did was because he had tenure," she said.

He then went into a succession of jobs, mostly driving trucks. And his house was a mess, his mother said.

"He began to think that Buffalo Bill was his great-grandfather. He was convinced that Frederick and I were not his real parents and he would demand to know who his real parents were. And his house distressed me terribly. It was so cluttered, so very cluttered. And dirty." Scott took care of that by burning the house down. A passer-by saw him take a lighted torch and throw it through a picture window.

"We got word of the fire and we went over. I thought that we would find him dead." Instead, Scott was standing in burned-out rubble.

"I didn't know what to do for him," his mother said, beginning to weep. "So on the way home, I had Frederick stop, and I bought Scott a toothbrush and toothpaste. Now, wasn't that a silly thing to do?"

Over the years, Ruth said, she had urged her son to see a counselor or a psychiatrist. He would have none of it. At one point he told his mother he was very depressed. She, not knowing very much about mental illness, said something like, "Well, Scott, it's winter time and you don't eat as many fresh fruits and vegetables in the winter as in the summer. Why don't you try taking some vitamins?"

"What a thing for a mother to do," she says sadly today. After the fire, for which he was later arrested, Scott insisted upon living in the burned-out shell of the house. His father gave him a Coleman stove, blankets, a tent, and other camping gear to try to make him more comfortable. Later, a friend of Scott refinished some of the inside of the house.

Meanwhile, his mental state was deteriorating. "I took him to lunch one day, and I will never forget that lunch as long as I live," his mother said. "All Scott did was talk about suicide, about how he'd never had one happy day in his whole life."

At the same time, he was hallucinating. He was sure his father was a headless man, he brought up the whole adoption thing again, and his mother noticed how angry he became when the car coughed as they were driving home.

The family decided he had to be hospitalized. Scott's sister made arrangements for him to go to St. Mary's in Lewiston, and the other sister came up from Massachusetts. The sisters went to see their brother. "We've come to take you for help," they said.

"Wait until I get my coat," Scott replied. He was ready for help.

St. Mary's ultimately decided that Scott should go to Togus Veterans Hospital outside Augusta. There, he was diagnosed as manic depressive and put on lithium. He also was transferred to the alcohol and drug rehabilitation unit.

"I look back on that as a wonderful time. Scott was sober, he was getting treatment and he was getting better," Ruth said. On weekends, he would come visit his parents and he and his mother would have wonderful talks.

"I cling so to those times," she said, her eyes filling again. "But he turned so against me at the end."

Scott was sent to the Maine Correctional Center at Windham after being hospitalized. His crimes were arson and growing marijuana in his backyard. "After that, he lost all hope," his mother said of the effects of being in prison.

Every time his parents went to see him, he was in maximum security. He would never say why, and neither would the prison officials. "He'd talk about how the food was good, how the guards were treating him well. But he'd never talk about himself," his mother said.

Frederick believes his son was fighting in prison. "There are a lot of men in prison who go in for homosexual activities. And Scott was always very proud of his body. He worked out a lot and everything. I think he was defending himself against homosexual advances."

Scott was sent to the pre-release center in Hallowell and his mother remembers in particular a visit she tried to make.

"I don't drive, so I took a taxi to Hallowell to see him. I had to wait the longest time for him to come out. And when he did, he said, 'Find someone else to visit, I'm tired.'" She had to go across the street and call the taxi driver to come back for her earlier than expected.

He was sent back to Windham for punching out his ex-wife's new husband, after breaking into their house in the middle of the night. He also did jail time for assaulting a doctor at Togus during a second stay there.

"He'd go off his medication, you see, and these things would happen."

Frederick has a hatred for doctors and he encouraged Scott not to take his pills. It was as if a real man did not need substances to be healthy. Today, Frederick regets his attitude. "I don't think my feelings toward doctors and drugs helped any."

The world, meanwhile, was closing in on Scott and his family. He called his mother in the middle of the night, told her everything she had done wrong as a parent and said he did not owe her a damn thing. A community service project that he was supposed to do in lieu of jail time fell through when he did not show up for the project. He got rid of his psychiatrist, fired his lawyer and decided to represent himself in future court cases. He also told his mother never to come see him again in jail.

Frederick found it easier to talk about objective subjects when he visited his son. "We'd talk about trucks or we'd joke and I'd try to make him laugh."

But the day would come when Scott would turn on his father.

"I can't tell you how I hated to answer the telephone," Ruth said. It was always bad news about Scott, another crisis, or another call from him, with his ranting. "I just always thought there could be a way I could help him. I was told to let go, but how can you?" Ruth said. It also is very difficult to let go when the mentally ill person's problems are all falling on you, all the bad news, all the messes, all the financial burden.

When Scott was released from jail in Auburn, his mother fixed a nice meal for him—special pork chops, baked potato, a home style meal. He was too agitated to eat, taking only a few mouthfuls.

A short time later he was committed to the Augusta Mental Health Institute, the last stop on the psychiatric trail as one worker there calls it.

It was there that Frederick found out how physically strong his son really was.

"I was sitting in the visitor's room, on a couch. And he came in and said he was going to take a few swings at me. He pinned me down and began punching me in the nose. Christ, there was blood all over the place. I didn't have a chance, I was just pinned down.

"But I'll have to say, he was a pretty good fighter. He never touched my glasses."

Staffers ran in and pulled Scott off his father. Frederick never went back to visit. But he was afraid the hospital would take the assault out on Scott.

"So I wrote a letter to the administration, saying it was just as much my fault as his, that I'd been too goddamn strict with him growing up and so on and so on."

He later spent a little more time in jail and was released on December 14, 1993. Three days later, he was dead.

He had marked off the dates of December 15, 16 and 17 on his calendar. His AA meditation book was lying by his chair with a telephone number written on the back.

His mother remembers how agitated he was when they drove him home from jail. "And I suppose the reason we didn't ask him to stay here was because we were afraid of him. We've never said it, but it's true. And why wouldn't we be afraid?"

On December 16, the parents received a call from a friend of Scott who was trying to reach him about an AA meeting. There was no answer, the friend said.

Frederick and Ruth went to Scott's house. His truck was there, there was a light on in the house, but no sign of him. His mother left a Christmas swag for his front door and a Christmas centerpiece.

I don't know if he ever got them or not," she said, crying. "He never knew how much we wanted him for Christmas. I just wanted one last Christmas with him. Was that so selfish?"

The parents went to the police who said they could have someone at Scott's house within a half hour, if necessary. The parents decided to wait one more day. "Now why did we do that?" Ruth asks.

"We knew something was wrong," she said. "I was so sure that he had taken his own life that I called a friend and said, 'I'm almost sure Scott is dead.'"

The next day, Ruth and Frederick went back and called the Sheriff's Department. Ruth noticed things in the house that did not seem right, like a large roll of picture framing wire. She stood inside the house, and before long, the deputies came back and she could hear them talking in hushed tones.

"And I knew they'd found him." He had hanged himself from a tree behind the house.

At first his mother did not want to see him, but Frederick took her hand and said, "You should look, Ruth. It might make you feel better."

"And there was utter, utter peace on his face. And I hadn't seen that for so many years," his mother said.

She asked that the Willie Nelson song "On the Road Again" be played at his memorial service, and sometime later, as family members were driving across the bridge in Augusta, they saw two eagles soaring in the sky, moving back and forth, back and forth.

"And I thought, Scott sent those two eagles, to tell us he's all right," Ruth said.

After a while, the parents felt relief that their son was at peace and the long family nightmare was over. "I just realized one day that a tremendous weight was gone," Scott's mother said.

"And I have no stigma about mental illness, or prison, or suicide. I suppose that has to do with my age."

Scott's ashes were scattered in the Berkshires in western Massachusetts, where he often said he wanted them to be. His father made the round trip one day to scatter them in a clearing.

"Did you cry? I'll bet you did," his wife said.

"I was doing a job. That's the way I saw it," her husband replied.

He Was Going to be Our College Grad

Andy Nasson seemed to be on the road to success when he was a youngster. He was bright, curious, outgoing and ambitious.

He was the youngest of William and Helen Nasson's three children and there were high hopes for him.

"He was going to be our first college grad," Helen said. "None of his older brothers went to college and we thought Andy would."

Instead, Andy never even received a high school diploma, because he could not concentrate well enough to study. When he was college age, his life was a succession of hospitalizations, entry-level jobs and long stretches of time living with his parents and making plans that never materialized.

"The latest plan is that he will go to Boston, get his own apartment and a job, and live there for the rest of his life," William said. "I predict that he will be back with us within three weeks."

William Nasson is a realist. He was in World War II and Korea, and knows what stress means, he said. His son has caused as much, or more, stress than combat, he stated.

William Nasson is in his sixties and has late on-set multiple sclerosis, a disease that usually affects people in their thirties or forties. Doctors have said stress caused William to develop the illness so late in life.

Andy's problems began in 1979, when he began his sophomore year in high school in Danvers, Massachusetts.

"He couldn't concentrate. He began getting poor grades. He had been an excellent student up until then. I thought of drugs, but that didn't seem to be the case," William said. "And he had had a slight head injury. But I think now that he was born with whatever he has."

Andy was tested at school for learning disabilities or other problems and nothing was found.

The first real episode came on a Sunday morning while the family was at breakfast. Andy began using irrational speech, speech that made no sense. His parents watched in horror as he became completely psychotic, breaking with reality right at the kitchen table.

"And that was it," his mother said. The first diagnosis was epilepsy. But anywhere from twenty to thirty doctors have diagnosed Andy as schizophrenic.

After the outbreak at the breakfast table, a judge ordered the boy committed to a hospital. His mother remembers going to see him.

"It was awful. He was in a ward with all these other people, wrapped in blankets. A whole row of patients wrapped in white blankets. Some of them were drooling, most of them couldn't speak."

Andy was put on Thorazine initially. He has since been on a number of medications, but often refuses to take them.

"He has had so many doctors and hospitals that we can't keep it all straight," his father said. "There have been seventeen or eighteen hospitalizations. He's been put in seclusion. He broke out of a hospital..." William said.

His job history is much the same story. "He has had jobs that lasted anywhere from twenty minutes to two and a half months. That last one was the longest. He gets frustrated, blows his top, and just walks off the job," his father said. "He will tell you he is a chef, but he's actually a dishwasher. Menial jobs."

One of the great tragedies of mental illness is the loss of potential. Many mentally ill people are very bright and have high aspirations. But their low stress levels prohibit them from working in jobs that meet their capacities. So the mentally ill are consigned to job training programs, where they take entry-level jobs at low wages.

Employers mean well when they take on people suffering from mental illness. But the jobs often do nothing for the former patient's already shaky self-esteem.

One restaurant owner in Augusta who has a mentally ill son will not hire the mentally ill to wash dishes or bus tables.

"In any restaurant, the dish washer is the lowest person on the totem pole, the one who is the butt of jokes, or is criticized. I won't subject mentally ill people to that," she said.

William and Helen Nasson, meanwhile, learned what so many other parents of mentally ill children come to learn: When things are going well, a fall is usually right around the corner.

"When he'd stay on his medication, he'd be rational. Then we'd have the rug pulled out from under us," Helen said. Their son would throw things around, smash furniture, stay up all night, and often take off on trips without warning.

"Without a nickel or a dime or a change of clothes, he'd take off. He's hitch-hiked all over New England," his father said.

After a few days, the call would come from Andy for his father to come pick him up. "I drove to every state except Connecticut."

William was doing all this while holding down a job with the State of Massachusetts. Some mornings he arrived at work without having had any sleep the night before.

"I told my supervisor that we had a problem at home, but that I would try not to let it affect my work. And as far as I know, it didn't."

William grew up in the downeast section of the state, in Machias,

Maine; Helen was from Boston and grew up in a poor family on Beacon Hill. The family had connections and a fine background, but no money, she said.

The couple moved back to Maine in 1986, a move that has created problems in getting help for Andy when he needs it.

"The services down here are terrible," Helen said. There is no full-time psychiatrist in Washington County, only one who visits one day a week from the next county. There are no crisis beds at either of the county's two small hospitals. No crisis services and only one branch of a counseling unit. For serious care or hospitalization, people must drive to Bangor one hundred miles away, where there are doctors, a state hospital, a private psychiatric hospital, and a large medical center.

"Down here, emergencies suddenly become non-emergencies," William said. He told of one time when Andy was agitated, psychotic and in need of help. His father took him to the local hospital emergency room.

"It took five hours for them to decide whether Andy should be taken to Bangor. It involved two doctors, a judge, the police," William said of the involuntary committal process.

When he was finally taken to Bangor Mental Health Institute by the police, the hospital refused to take him because he did not pose a danger to himself or others, doctors there decided. So Andy was taken to Acadia Hospital, a private facility in Bangor.

Helen feels great pity for her son. "He wants to be normal and have a normal job."

She also saw all his friends fall away after he became sick in high school. "It was so sad. I had a birthday party for him one year, I think it was his sixteenth birthday, and only one person came." I said to him, "Andy, at least you know you have that one friend."

She said he makes lists of all the girls he would like to date. "He talks all the time about how he wants to get married."

The lists of girls are ones he knew in high school, years ago, before he became sick. They are, of course, in their thirties now and probably all married.

"He thinks he has a lot of friends," his mother said. "Even though he's not an alcoholic, he goes to AA to meet people."

"The truth is," William said, "he has one person in Maine and one in Massachusetts who will tolerate him. That's all. Tolerate him."

In his book *Fates Worse Than Death*, Kurt Vonnegut calls the mentally ill the "World Champions of Loneliness." What he is talking about are the differences that set the mentally ill apart from others. People with mental illness often talk too much, in an incoherent way. They take up too much of other people's space. They are unpredictable in their actions. Nobody seems to understand their thoughts.

As happened with Andy, friends drop away, especially when the ill person is a teenager. Other kids make fun of the person, or think it is not cool to befriend a mentally ill classmate.

So the sick person goes into a shell, feeling with all sensitivity the forces of rejection and stigma, while at the same time longing for friends.

Helen is her son's friend, but she tires of the job. "I talk to him, because everyone else rejects him. But sometimes, I just feel like shouting, 'Get out of my face!'"

William is more likely to retreat behind the newspaper when his son gets going. "I just shut up," he said.

"There have been some differences of opinion in how to deal with him," he said when asked about tension between the parents.

And both parents said they have wished their son would just die and get it over with. "We've never said much about it out loud, but, yes, we have felt that way," William said.

That may sound shocking to people who have not dealt with a mentally ill family member. But the toll such illnesses take on families and the constant stress about what is going to happen next create a home full of chaos and despair.

One mother in Portland has a mentally ill daughter. She also had a son die in a freak accident while on the job. When asked which was worse, having the mentally ill child or losing a child, she said the mental illness was harder. Death, she said, is a terrible thing at the time, but it is final. Having a mentally ill family member is a living death, she said, because it goes on and on, and no one knows when or how it will end.

Andy Nasson has been in group homes, in boarding homes, and at home with his parents. Group homes did not work out, mainly because he would not be responsible for taking his medication. He often would just up and leave the homes, too.

His mother knows the tension of living with his illness all too well. At one point, he went after her with a knife.

"He became agitated, threatening. He threw a lamp, then he came after me with a large kitchen knife. I ran into the bathroom and locked the door. He plunged the knife right through the panel in the door. I was so scared. I jumped into the bathtub, that was the only thing I could think of to do. Here was this knife halfway through the door," she said.

As soon as he did that, she said, he ran off into the woods behind the house. "That's what he does. He'll do something and then he'll run away."

The couple has learned to tell when it is time for Andy to go to the hospital. He begins to pace and becomes agitated, a common symptom of someone who is on the verge of an episode. Then his behavior becomes more and more extreme, until his father talks him into going for help.

The Nassons were devastated when their son was diagnosed as mentally ill. They knew nothing about such illness, although William said he has a sister "who isn't all there." The parents also had nowhere to turn, until they went to a clinic run by Massachusetts General Hospital. Andy was given every test available and the answer was schizo-affective disorder with paranoia.

"He does not yet fully appreciate his condition," the father said. That is why Andy goes off his medications, he said. "Mentally, he is still fifteen," the age he was when the illness struck.

It is normal for mentally ill people to become stuck in the age they were when they became sick. Years of hospitalizations and lack of contact with the real world contribute to this retarded development. And the brain is going through such a frenzy working overtime just to cope with the disease, that there is little energy or rationality left over for social development.

Helen has been helped by a twelve-step recovery program and by her Unitarian faith in coping with her son's illness. The Unitarians, she said, have a spirituality that appeals to her, and members of that faith have a welcoming approach to the mentally ill.

William relies upon his own survival skills, the ones he picked up through life, the ones that served him through two wars, and now are serving him through this personal one.

The two rarely have a vacation together. They can leave Andy for two or three days, but they usually come back to find that he has not eaten, that he has damaged something, that there has been a problem. He is never far from their minds, even if they try to skip away for a few days.

William had done some writing that has been published. But the whole experience with Andy has killed his desire to write. He's just too tired and pre-occupied.

"I don't know where I would be without this. I'm just so weary. I know I don't have the urge to publish anymore," he said.

Helen is trying to detach from her son, with love. "He's got to find his own way," she said. Yet she knows that way will be very hard, fraught with anger, for someone like Andy.

"We no longer worry about what will happen to him after we're gone," William said. "We stopped worrying about that a year ago. I will just have to let someone else worry about that."

What Did We Get for $18 Million?

Scott Brousseau was a patient at the Augusta Mental Health Institute during the summer of 1988, the year five people at the hospital died in one of the hottest summers on record.

There was no air conditioning, only a few fans that patients sat near trying to cool off. "The hospital was extremely overcrowded," Brousseau remembered. "People's medical conditions weren't taken care of—I mean their physical conditions," he said.

"We had that awful heat," he continued. "I mean, those bricks just held the heat. Some of the patients were in seclusion, as they call it, without food or water," Brousseau, in his thirties, said.

Other patients were in restraints. And nobody paid much attention at the time. One man died of heat stroke while struggling in restraints, fighting so hard that his artificial eye popped out and flew across the room. Minutes later, his heart gave out.

The deaths, all attributed to heat, spurred a state investigation that went on for months. Yet questions still are unanswered after all these years.

Augusta Mental Health Institute was built in the 1840's as an asylum for Maine's insane population. The plans called for a three hundred bed hospital, because it was thought that only that many people at a time would require treatment. Care initially consisted of rest and time.

But the hospital grew, both in the number of buildings and in the number of patients. At one point in the 1950's, and in previous years, there were as many as seventeen hundred patients. Not all were mentally ill. Many were alcoholic, or just poor, or simply lacked anywhere else to go.

All patients were housed together and there were no wards for special treatment. The only drugs were Thorazine and minor tranquilizers, such as Valium. When dozens of patients were released under deinstitutionalization in the early 1970's, many were found to have been confined for three or four decades, for no clear reason.

One man was there for forty years after suffering a mild breakdown in the 1930's. He was an artist whose family deserted him and whose wife later divorced him. He had no advocate. Today he is a well-known painter in the Augusta area.

The conditions and deaths in 1988 sparked fury and a barrage of questions. Some three hundred and sixty patients were in buildings designed for three hundred and thirty. The state at that time required no licensing of space, so Augusta Mental Health Institute was free to take as many patients as staff felt it could handle.

After that summer, some patients and their families had had enough. Eleven patients filed suit, asking that hospital conditions be made more humane, that AMHI be cleaned up physically, and that community services be put into place to accommodate former patients.

Patients were being dumped into towns and cities with no place to live, no network of services, and little follow-up care. A number of the mentally ill wound up on the streets, sick and alone.

Brousseau, a manic depressive, is a member of the original suit, which later became known at the AMHI consent decree after a settlement between the state and the plaintiffs was reached in 1990.

The original decree, more than one hundred pages long, spells out everything from the use of restraints to the need for individual support plans for patients leaving AMHI.

The suit has grown to represent three thousand and three hundred past and present patients, anyone who was at AHMHI during or after 1988.

But after five years and eighteen million dollars spent on the decree, what has been accomplished? Some say not much, others say a little.

"For me, it's given me some sense of control over my life," said Brousseau who has his own apartment and is on the Governor's Mental Health Advisory Committee. He also helps the mentally ill speak up for themselves.

Those skills proved valuable in the summer of 1994 when Brousseau admitted himself to Augusta Mental Health Institute after a suicide attempt. He is a large man who can become violent or agitated when manic. But for his first three days at the hospital, records show, nurses found him to be in control and not difficult to manage.

On the fourth day a visiting doctor declared a medical emergency, insisting that Brousseau be given heavy doses of Haldol, a sedative, and Ativan, a highly addictive tranquilizer used to quell anxiety. The doctor ordered the medications based on Brousseau's prior history and to avoid any potentially violent behavior.

According to the records and the Maine Advocacy Services, a legal and lobbying group for the disabled, Brousseau had shown no signs of violent or assaultive behavior. The medication was not necessary.

But nurses who had dealt with Brousseau in the past told the doctor about his history. The psychiatrist treating Brousseau decided his patient was in danger of a full-blown manic episode.

Brousseau was forcefully given medication through injection, a violation of hospital policy if it is given against the patient's wishes. Brousseau complained that the doses were too high and that other medication, such as Lithium, had worked better for him in the past. He was put into seclusion, where, the nurse's report says, he did nothing but sleep. He also was on constant suicide watch, even though he was so groggy and his speech so slurred, when an advocate went to see him that it is unlikely Brousseau could have harmed himself.

Maine Advocacy Services went to bat for Brousseau after he called the agency. The agency was told by the doctor that Brousseau was being treated as he was in part because he contacted outside advocates.

The same doctor also referred to his patient as a "poster boy for mental illness," because Brousseau had done a public service announcement of such illness.

The nurses who witnessed the abuse of Brousseau were found to be too intimidated by the doctors to question the practices being used. Under the patients' bill of rights, Brousseau had the right to refuse medication, to call an advocate and not have his past records discussed with a new doctor.

The hospital later apologized to Brousseau and took steps to ensure that such incidents became less frequent, but they still do happen.

It is this kind of thing that Maine's former and present mental health commissioners want to correct, along with inadequate housing, poverty, lack of crisis services, lack of beds outside of Augusta Mental Health Institute, and lack of community support teams.

Melodie Peet, Maine's mental health commissioner, envisions a series of six regional mental health centers where people can go if they need medication, counseling, or other aid. Without this, she said, individual patients will not be served and there will be no point of contact for the state.

"We have too many of some services and not enough of others," she said. "There is no organization in any region for finding AMHI class members of meeting services. We've gone about setting up elements of programs, but there's no umbrella for individual plans," she said.

Peet says the state can come into compliance with the consent decree without a huge infusion of money. What is needed, she said, is better planning. But the court master, who oversees the decree, disagrees. He thinks more funding is needed.

Peet's budget for the decree calls for about thirty million dollars for 1996 and 1997, about two million dollars less than that presented by former commissioner Sue Davenport. Many think the former commissioner went for broke in submitting so large a budget, because Davenport knew she would never spend that much. The Legislature would have shot it down. So the figure became merely an intellectual exercise designed to placate the court.

The consent degree, meanwhile, has languished for five years since being signed in 1990. It has been underfunded because of a state budget crisis, with only eighteen million dollars spent on it so far. At the same time, the mental health department has had three commissioners in five years.

Jamie Morril, Peet's assistant, said he cannot say today where the eighteen million went.

"I honestly don't know. We can't get a handle on that. It may very well be that the money was ill-spent on a fragmented system," he said. "It's a very good question. What did we get for $18 million?"

Brousseau got forced injections of high dosage drugs; Mark LaValle, another person with mental illness, was unable to get his teeth fixed; hundreds of others became such pests on the streets that the cities of Portland, Bangor, and several towns in southern Maine sued the state for better conditions.

A judge ruled that the state had an obligation to care for its mentally ill whether the patients were covered by the AMHI consent decree or not. The ruling has set up a dilemma for the state. Not only must it provide care and services for those who have been at Augusta Mental Health Institute, it also is responsible for another seven thousand mentally ill from all corners of Maine.

The AMHI decree covers former patients from Augusta to the tip of southern Maine. The other ruling affects mostly people in northern and eastern Maine. That area is served by another state hospital, Bangor

Mental Health Institute. That hospital is not under court decree to carry out any mandates.

The fear is that those not covered by the AMHI decree will be left out for lack of funding, and that a two-tier system of mental health will emerge in Maine. One for the haves, and one for the have-nots.

Even the director of the Alliance for the Mentally Ill of Maine has called the AMHI decree "a disaster," because it has the potential to take huge chunks of money from other mental health accounts.

While the AMHI decree will receive as much as thirty million dollars during the next two years, others with mental illness may see as little as ten million for their needs.

Peet said the problem statewide is a piecemeal system that has had money thrown at it with no real plan in mind. "Previous attempts have had no method for pulling things together. Everything has been an applique, added on," she said.

She rejected the community plan submitted by Davenport in 1994 and decided to do her own plan. The move delayed legislative approval for funding until the court master for the consent decree approved Peet's plan. The court master, in turn, took several weeks on his recommendations, then gave a lukewarm endorsement, saying more money was needed.

Peet, during the next two years, wants to build a strong system of services, then release more patients from Augusta Mental Health Institute by closing two wards and cutting more than two hundred and twenty-five jobs at the state hospital. That is the opposite of what has been done in the past, when patients were released before the state figured out what to do with them.

At least one national study shows Maine ranking fourth in the nation in per patient spending for mental illness, but that is misleading, because it overlooks the fact that Maine is still driven by institutional care, which costs six hundred dollars per day per patient.

"We've had an over-reliance on hospitalization," the commissioner said. "We can't keep doing that, because if we do, we'll do it forever," she said.

State figures show about sixty percent of the state mental health budget goes to the two state hospitals, the rest goes to community services. Not too long ago, less than thirty percent went into the community.

The Legislature right now is talking seriously about closing one or both of its antiquated, expensive hospitals and building one small new one, to house forensic patients and those who are too sick ever to be released.

The small hospital would be located either on AMHI or Bangor grounds and would hold about sixty patients. The cost savings in maintenance, salaries, and other bills would eventually pay for the new facility. Right now most of Augusta Mental Health Institute is shut down, with many of the old buildings used as state offices. The hospital could use one million dollars worth of repairs and maintenance each year, money that is not available and, some say, would be a waste.

Peet, meanwhile, began her tenure in the winter of 1995 by firing five top officials, including the superintendent of Augusta Mental Health Institute. But, Peet has promised to meet the 1997 compliance date for the consent decree, a deadline set by the court in a contempt finding in September of 1994.

At that time, Justice Bruce Chandler, now retired, found the state in contempt, accusing state officials of neglect, laziness, indifference, and just plain arrogance in its approach to the 1990 decree.

While he sympathized with the state's lack of funds, he said that was no excuse for doing nothing. As a result of his ruling, deadlines were set, the compliance date was moved from 1995 to 1997, and the state got the message to go into action.

To make sure it did, Chandler said if necessary, the court would take money from other mental health accounts to fund the consent decree. The state has appealed that section of the court order, arguing that only the governor and the Legislature can allocate funds and move money around.

Peet's plan calls for housing (with rental assistance), crisis services, more support teams, and the use of community hospitals for severely ill mental patients who need hospitalization.

She would free up nearly one million dollars to help community hospitals one time with funding for the psychiatric patients. Local hospitals can use the patients and the money. Most hospitals in Maine average a fifty percent capacity on any given day, as more and more procedures are done on an out-patient basis and patients are sent home from hospitals earlier than they used to be. Peet's funding for the next two years depends upon about ten to

sixteen million dollars from the state, money that would come from shifting accounts because Governor Angus King said no new money could be used for the AMHI decree. The mental health department also wants a four million dollar bond put out to referendum in the fall, asking for housing and other facilities for the mentally ill. The rest of the money would come from Medicaid. It is a shaky package.

And in the meantime the mentally ill wait for the end of discrimination and stigma.

Brousseau said he was getting better at Augusta Mental Health Institute last summer before the doctor over-medicated him. "I just wasn't getting better fast enough for them," he said.

The mentally ill "are the most disenfranchised group of individuals in our society, at the bottom of the social class structure," he said.

I Felt Like a Circus Freak

The walls and ceiling in Jared Fiori's bedroom would stretch and contort, forming faces with mouths open screaming in anguish.

"It was my anguish they were expressing," said Jared, a seventeen year old from Monmouth who was so terrified by the hallucinations that they drove his already troubled mind to the brink of suicide.

During his sophomore year in high school, he slashed his wrists deeply, both across a vein and up the arm. He meant business.

"I had a whole chest full of knives that I had been collecting, everything from small knives to machetes. I was on the mailing list for three cutlery magazines," he said.

The night he slashed his wrist, he went into the shower, where he bled into the water, then lay in a fetal position in the tub for about a half hour. He wrapped a towel around his wrists, drenching the towel in blood.

"Then I looked in the mirror and I saw what I thought I was, and I put my fist through the mirror," he said. When he returned to his room, the blood from his wrist and had soaked the bed and sheets.

His father found him just as Jared was putting a machete to his throat.

The boy was rushed to the hospital, where he spent twenty-eight days and was diagnosed as having depression, a personality disorder, paranoia, and morbidity.

The morbidity showed up early in life. Jared has an exceptionally high IQ, which he will not reveal, but he probably approaches the genius range. At the same time, he is intensely sensitive, to the point that as a child he gave human qualities to inanimate objects.

"Empty shells abandoned on the beach would make me sad. They were different, not like other shells. We had an abandoned tree house in our front yard, and I couldn't go near it. I thought of the memories and the happiness that had taken place there and I couldn't stand it. My parents thought it would make a nice tree house for us, with a little work, but I wanted nothing to do with it," he said.

Jared's problems began in third grade, when his family moved to Maine. His father had abandoned the family, leaving Jared's mother with four young children. He thinks that feeling of being left alone is linked to his sorrow over objects and places that seem rejected.

"I was definitely more sensitive than others. I always had intricate funerals for birds that died near our house. My family would say, oh, it's just a bird, but I would mourn very deeply."

Jared talks like someone far older than his years and his insights are very mature. Those qualities made him feel isolated at school as a small child, for he could not talk on the same level as the other younger children. "I told myself I was lazy. It was better than being weird or depressed." His mother took him to a counselor who, after two months, threw up his hands and said he could not help the child.

"He said I had an inordinately high IQ, but no productivity," Jared said. Nothing was said about childhood depression.

"For a third grade child to confuse a Ph.D., is pretty unfathomable, don't you think?" he asks.

The child was very lonely, very unhappy. "No one liked to talk with me. My jokes were on a higher plane. I wanted to converse with other kids, but I couldn't lower my intellect."

It was at that time he first thought of suicide. He was too young to make the connection between cutting oneself and bleeding to death, but he tied his hands to the bed posts and pulled with all his strength, until he shut off his circulation. At least he knew he could do something self-destructive, something to ease the pain inside.

He attended three elementary schools growing up. His mother remarried twice, both times unsuccessfully. Her fourth marriage worked and Jared was thrilled. "I had prayed so for a father. And I got a dad. He had no children from his former marriage, and the day he married my mother, he instantly inherited five children from her former marriages. He did really well with us," Jared said.

When Jared was in fourth and fifth grades, the bullies began taunting him, making him paranoid and terribly scared.

"There was this one boy and his back-up pal. They followed me to my house. They were at the same bus stop. They were everywhere I was. I dreaded going to school. And I'd arrange to get to the bus stop just as the bus was about to take off."

He was threatened, bothered in the cafeteria, and petrified. "I was frightened by their ignorance. Ignorance plus power is a dangerous thing," he said.

In fourth grade, he had a following of students who hung around him. "They were not friends. They were just intrigued by me. I felt like a circus freak to them."

Jared was selected for the school's gifted and talented program, but says now he received little enrichment from it. Two years later, he was held back in seventh grade, a blunder on the part of school officials. All research show that children should not be held back in school at that late a time, because it does little except damage an already wounded self-esteem.

There were other counselors as Jared went through school, one who worked with the whole family and said the boy needed less structure and more respect at home. "It worked for awhile," he said. "But eventually I just became isolated. My parents didn't know when to leave me alone to work things out, and when to talk things out with me."

"And I was very hard on myself, very self-punishing. If something went wrong, I always blamed myself."

He hated being labeled depressed. "I said, don't put me in a file cabinet of illnesses."

His thoughts of suicide became more intense. He spent hours on top of the family's barn, trying to get up the nerve to jump. "And I internalized everything. If a friend had a problem, I obsessed about it. Trying to deal with other people's problems along with my own pushed me right over the edge," he said.

He developed two other personalities as a way to cope with what was going on around him. He has no memory of the other personalities, but has been told by others of their emergence.

"One was a very Gothic character who spoke in Shakespearean language, calling people "Duchess" and "Sir Knight." This person was royal, from the Middle Ages. The other person was Tony. Tony was a jerk with a tough-guy accent."

He also was violent. As Tony, Jared once hit his brother across the back with a bicycle chain. "I don't remember anything about it, yet there are the scars on my brother's back," he said. "I am not a violent person at all. I hate violence!"

Tony also punched out kids at school, while the Gothic character spread love and good feelings.

It was around this time that the walls and ceilings began to move in his bedroom and, once, in the principal's office at Monmouth Academy. The Principal looked distorted as well and Jared began talking in irrational speech that lacked lucidity.

The principal excused himself and never came back. Jared grabbed a pair of scissors from the principal's desk, stabbed himself in the wrist, and went to the lunchroom and punched out a kid.

The school sent him home for the day.

"That is their way of dealing with things. They would rather dismiss a student than deal with the real problems," he said. The school has no counselor for such crises and little patience for such actions.

Monmouth Academy is the public high school for the town of Monmouth. It prides itself on image, high statewide test scores and the number of students who go on to college.

It is very strong academically and has a statewide reputation for excellence. But it fails students like Jared.

"I was supposed to be a normal kid. I don't think high statewide test scores mean squat. I think that means conformity, going along with what they want," Jared said.

The school has had other mentally ill students pass through its halls, and most have dropped out or transferred to other schools, which is ultimately what Jared did.

When Jared returned to Monmouth after slashing his wrist, he was told that he would probably flunk all his subjects because he was incomplete as a result of hospitalization.

"That didn't help my depression at all," he said. He made up some of his work and took a correspondence course in English to receive that credit.

The wrist-slashing was not Jared's first path to the hospital. Earlier, he swallowed two hundred and fifty over-the-counter pain killers, gulping them down with a large jar of water. He then stumbled to the attic of the garage and waited to pass out.

His parents, who were away from the house at the time, had a premonition that something was wrong and returned home. They found Jared, but he would not tell his folks what he had taken, nor would he tell the paramedics when they arrived. His father finally found the half-empty bottle of pills.

"They loaded me into an ambulance, and by the time I got to the hospital, my liver was about to shut down," he said. He spent three weeks in the hospital, was given an excellent psychiatrist, and put on an anti-depressant. The medication did not work. It worsened his mood swings and disturbed his already mixed-up sleeping patterns.

"Medications are like colognes," Jared said. "You can find one that smells great in the store, but when you put it on yourself, it stinks. And one that stinks in the store can be just right for you," he said. He was switched to Prozac which has worked quite well.

When he was released from the hospital, the school principal said, "You're out of the hospital now, so you should be all set to return to school."

That is not the way it works. Hospitals treat the acute stage of the illness and stabilize the patient. But there is a recuperation period that follows, sometimes lasting weeks or months, just as there is when one is recovering from any illness.

With mental illness, the brain has been through a firestorm and it needs a rest, peace and quiet. The former patient can have bad days, or at the very least, sleep a great deal. A wise school will arrange tutoring or a modified schedule for a student coming out of the hospital.

The second time Jared was hospitalized, Monmouth Academy sent all his homework to his ward, saying, this is what you must do over the next three weeks.

"I couldn't get any work done," he said. "My mind was so confused, I couldn't concentrate."

He was becoming more and more behind in school, his grades were not good, and he became a discipline problem. "I walked out of class, I would lose coherence. I learned faster than the other students and I hated waiting for them," he said. So he would leave class out of frustration.

One teacher, Jared's French teacher, understood. She has taught at the school for nearly thirty five years and is greatly loved by the students. She formed a bond with Jared, and often could see psychotic symptoms coming on before he could.

Once she had him make a list of all the good things about himself, a list of affirmations. She did the same thing and turned it into a kind of game or competition.

"I still have that list on my bedroom wall, and I look at it whenever I feel the need to," Jared said.

Jared's bedroom is a kind of shrine to spirituality. His family are Mormons and Jared has a deep belief in God and the ability of a higher power to help him. His room has posters with messages like, "The Telephone Line to God is Never Busy." He also has a drafting table in his room, for his art work, and a bookcase full of neatly placed paperbacks on all subjects. There are a few vases of flowers and other objects designed to keep the spirits up.

"I'm not sure depression is a mental illness," he said. "It's what you do with it. During the bad times I try to ride it out, knowing that it will go away."

Yet two weeks before saying that, he clung to a metal pole on a metal bridge during a lightning storm, hoping he would be struck.

"I don't want to die," he said. "I just want to stop the pain. Suicide is a means to the end of the pain." He is talking about internal pain, an anguish that overwhelms its victims, bringing on the desire for an endless sleep to alleviate the unbearable discomfort.

Some have described depression as having a helmet over their heads, or a veil that somehow cannot be lifted.

At the beginning of Jared's junior year in high school, the principal suggested that he go to an alternative school in Turner, in another school system. Monmouth would pay the tuition since it has no alternative program of its own.

"I think he was just tired and sick of dealing with me," Jared said.

The Turner school, about twenty miles from Monmouth, was founded for students who could not cope with the regular school schedule or with a large high school. Its purpose is to prevent students from dropping out of school.

Students plan a course of study, then are given flexible hours for when they will attend class. Some go in the morning, some in the afternoon.

One of the former teachers at the school, Bill Nave, was named Maine's Teacher of the Year in 1991 and was one of four finalists that year for the national teacher award.

Jared has blossomed in the less structured environment. The school also offers his only hope for graduating on time, for he can work at his own pace and meet minimum credits. He still goes to Monmouth Academy every other day for French.

But Jared is worried. Monmouth wants to start its own alternative program in 1995-1996, and he is afraid the school will insist that he attend it. "It will just be getting started, and I am doing well at Turner. But Monmouth might say they don't want to pay the tuition for me to continue at Turner," he said. Jared's parents can pay the tuition, of course, or they can make a case that he belongs in the other school district because it is in his best interest to continue there.

Jared said his parents still worry about suicide attempts, especially because he sleeps from four o'clock in the afternoon to one a.m., then gets up and does homework, his art projects, and putters around the house.

"They worry about suicide attempts constantly," he said. "They are heavy sleepers and they're afraid they wouldn't hear me if I did anything."

He also has been appointed to a statewide task force on teen-age suicide in Maine, which has an adolescent suicide rate eighteen percent above the national average. Of males between the ages of thirteen and twenty-four, some twenty-eight out of every one thousand take their own lives. For the same age group, eight girls of every one thousand do.

Girls are more likely to attempt suicide, but they are less successful, because they use pills. Boys are more likely to use guns or knives.

And among the mentally ill, the rate of suicide for all ages is twenty-five percent higher than for the rest of the population.

He has no social life, mainly because of his sleeping routine. He goes home from school, has something light to eat, then goes to bed. He finds the wee hours of the morning the perfect time for projects and work, a time when no one else is around and he is undisturbed.

"Currently I'm happy," he said. "I am secretly engaged. I think I want to go to college and teach art, for art is one of the best cures for depression."

But the threat and fear is always there for family members and desperation never lurks too far beneath the surface for those with profound mental disorders.

It was a Very Volatile House

Susan Dore remembers her mother sitting in church, wearing a gorgeous broad-brimmed hat and elegant gloves that stretched above her elbows.

Susan, about four years old at the time, knew her mother was beautiful.

"But I also knew she was a fragile China doll," said Dore, forty, who is a legislator from Auburn. "I knew she was a vulnerable person who had to be taken care of."

As she talks, Dore is sitting in a white rocking chair on the veranda of the State House. She sits on the edge of the chair, speaking with an intensity that indicates this is the first time she has gone public with her story, the story of what it is like to have a parent with mental disease.

Not only did Dore as a child sense that there was something different about her mother, she also sensed there was something different about the way her family lived. Nobody ever visited the home that Dore, her two sisters and mother shared with Dore's grandparents.

The family seemed to have money, but there was frugality, with the children wearing hand-me-down clothes and brushing their teeth with salt to save on toothpaste.

And usually each fall and spring, Dore's mother would be gone for weeks at a time. People would be told she was away visiting.

By the time Susan was eight years old, she had figured out the truth. Her mother was mentally ill. She had manic depression, a mood disorder.

"I remember seeing her burn all her clothes in the fireplace. And I knew then that this was not normal," Susan said.

Dore was the sponsor of legislation that brought insurance coverage for mental illness to the same level as other illnesses. The bill was signed into law once, in 1993, but with a sunset provision that meant it had to be re-enacted or voted on again in 1995. It passed easily.

There was no insurance for treatment of mental illness when Susan's mother was receiving private care at a hospital in Bangor, Uterback's.

"There was always a sense that there was a financial crisis," Susan said. All the money earned by the grandparents, Tom and Irene Simpson, was put aside for the next hospitalization.

Major insurance companies now will cover a portion of hospital stays and outpatient treatment for psychiatric care, but the percentage is still only half what it is for other diseases in many cases, and the lifetime cap for mental illness expenses in Maine is now $100,000.

For heart disease or other disorders, the cap can go as high as one million dollars, or can be unlimited. Under Maine's new law, the limits will be the same for mental illness.

"I know at times that my grandparents had anywhere from $25,000 to $30,000 in the bank," Susan said. "But it all had to be saved for the next time my mother was sick."

Her mother spent nine months at Augusta Mental Health Institute as a young woman. When she was released, Dore's grandmother swore she would never put her daughter in the state hospital again.

"So life became focused on keeping Marge out of the state hospital and having Marge keep her family," Susan said. There was a real danger that the state could have taken the children.

Dore's father abandoned the family when the girls were small. The only solution, given the mother's instability, was to move in with the grandparents.

The grandmother, who is now ninety, took over the care and discipline of the family, assuming almost a masculine role, Susan recalled. Her grandmother made the family decisions and handled the finances. She made draperies as a way of earning money.

The grandfather, a carpenter and contractor, was softer, often giving the girls money for treats. "One year, he gave us all bicycles," Susan said. "It was so beautiful. Three new bicycles line up on Christmas morning."

As a young child, Susan saw her mother as a victim of the grandmother's domination. Later Susan came to see that her mother needed constant care and attention.

"There was no peace. It was a very volatile household," Susan said. "There just wasn't enough mother to go around. My grandmother didn't have time," Dore says today.

"There were a couple of times, though, when I really needed my mother and she was there for me," Susan said. Once was when Susan's first boyfriend broke up with her. She was about fourteen and devastated.

"I called my mother from school, crying. And she said, 'Come home and I'll fix a warm bath for you,'" Susan said.

Her mother's illness was kept secret, except from a very few people. The children felt the stigma of having a sick mother who consumed most of their grandmother's time. "We were kids in a middle class neighborhood in Auburn, in a beautiful house that my grandfather built. But we had some very poor things about us," Susan said.

No brownies were baked for the Parent/Teacher Club, the children wore second-hand clothes and sometimes went to school not dressed warmly enough.

"We felt like freaks," Susan said of herself and her two sisters. "Everybody in that house was stuck."

Susan remembers the warning signals when her mother was becoming sick. She would dress all in black and wear far too much mascara and other make-up. Her sleeping patterns would be off, and she might smoke obsessively or eat only one thing obsessively. And her hands would shake terribly.

No one in the house rested well when the mother was up at night. There was fear, fear of what she might do. Sometimes she took off, even to other states, and the family waited for a call to come pick her up.

"It's a sickening kind of fear," Susan said of that kind of fear felt by a child.

Her grandparents, she said, often waited too long to take her mother to the hospital, because of the money. And hospital treatment in the 1960's was mostly uppers and downers and electroshock therapy. Lithium was yet to be used for such illnesses.

The circumstances took a toll on each of the children.

"I just felt so sad all the time. It was relentless, that sadness. I was so afraid I might have my mother's illness."

Often she would stay away from home, going to friends' houses, or seeking solace in the woods behind the house. She rode her bike for miles, to escape emotional pain.

When Susan was ten, her mother remarried, and Susan went to

live with her mother and stepfather. The marriage produced a son, but lasted only three years. "It was a very unhealthy house, a violent house," she said. "He drank, and she drank to keep up with him."

She will say no more about those years.

When she was thirteen, Dore and her sisters were officially adopted by Susan's grandparents. The half-brother was raised by his father's parents.

By this time, Susan had lost interest in school. She excelled in government and English, but was more interested in the anti-Vietnam War movement than anything else.

"I was a draft counselor by the time I was fifteen. I was this mouthy kid who had a mission to make the world just. I wanted external order because there was no order in my internal life."

She was seeing a counselor at a mental health center who helped her realize that she was not responsible for her mother's illness. She also read up on manic depression and through that reading found out about lithium, a drug for mood disorders.

"When I was a senior in high school, I took home some literature and I said, 'This is what Mom has. And this is what they give for it,'" she said.

Her mother's long-time doctor thought lithium was too new, too experimental. So Susan's mother went to the real mental health center and got a prescription.

"And she had fifteen glorious years," Susan said. "She became a wonderful grandmother, she even took a few college courses. It was wonderful to see her in the role she could be good in."

During those years, Susan married, at the age of twenty. Her husband is several years older than she and is now an attorney in Lewiston.

"I wanted nothing to do with college-age boys, with their beer parties and their antics. I had seen enough of that," she said. A few years after her marriage, she graduated from the Unversity of Southern Maine.

"I was a very old young woman. I knew things about people that kids normally are sheltered from," she said.

Seven years ago, the lithium stopped working for Susan's mother. She then spent most of three years in St. Mary's General Hospital in

Lewiston. There were suicide attempts as the medication lost its effectiveness. "How do you tell your two children whose grandmother seemed to love them so much, that she wanted to leave them?" Susan asked.

"Oh, God, I was angry. I was devastated," she said of the series of relapses. Apartments and boarding houses for her mother failed, and Dore's grandparents, in failing health, were unable to care for their daughter anymore.

The mother, now sixty-five, is in a private group home and is on the medication Clozaril.

Susan shows two pictures of her mother. One shows a lovely young woman with full lips, dark eyes and long wavy hair. The other is of a woman ravaged by mental illness, her hair undone and sticking out, her eyes vacant, her face puffy.

"It's painful to look at these," said Susan who said the experience with her mother taught her that children can overcome anything.

"This was a horrible tragedy that happened to all of us. But you can survive. You have to turn it into a force for change. I have a hunger to be happy. I have a hunger not to be sad a moment beyond what is necessary. I have spent enough of my life being sad."

She Was Quite a Lady

In the middle of the night last winter, Alex James, unable to sleep, left her Brewer apartment and walked a mile up the street to a convenience store.

When she casually mentioned the pre-dawn stroll to an acquaintance the next day, the woman told James to be careful about wandering out alone at night.

"I'm not scared," James reportedly said. "There's nothing out there that's going to bother you."

On the afternoon of June 16, James was seen leaving her South Main Street apartment for the last time. Sometime between eight p.m. that

Friday and seven a.m. Saturday, James who suffered from mental illness, was brutally murdered, her body left in an industrial park five miles from Brewer.

Murder is still rare enough in the Bangor-Brewer community to prompt big headlines and days of coffee shop talk. But the randomness of the attack on fifty-eight year old Alex added a new dimension to conversation and the concern of the community.

Detectives in Maine investigate an average of twenty-five homicides a year. Unlike elsewhere in the country, Maine investigators usually do not have to look further than the victim's back yard to find the killer.

In the case of Alex James, police are still unsure who committed the grisly crime, which has left a sense of uneasiness in the Bangor area. It was not the sort of crime police in Maine often have to deal with, and Alex was not an average victim.

For nearly half her life, Alex suffered in varying degrees from a mental condition that left her wary of people and unable to drive.

A former English teacher, a mother of two highly successful sons, Alex was once known as an All-American country girl who was raised in an active farm family in Sangerville.

But by the time she died, her illness had left her confined, physically and emotionally, to a world much smaller than the one she had planned for herself as a young girl.

She would venture out on foot or on a city bus for the day, and then return, always alone, to her modest apartment. Unlike in her youth, there were no friends to play cards with, no children or pets to nurture.

After living nearly sixty years, Alex had only two or three people who knew her life story from beginning to end.

"She was quite a lady," said her ex-husband, Drummond Easley, Jr. "But she did have a very serious problem for many, many years."

He did not say what it was, but the signs point to schizophrenia.

Alex James was born as Joy Crafts in December of 1936 in Sangerville, the only girl among Clair and Lelia Crafts' four children.

Their small family farm was bolstered by the incomes of both parents who worked in the Guilford Industries mill nearby. Though money was tight, Lelia Crafts was determined that all four children, all exceptionally bright and close in age, would attend college.

According to interviews with relatives and former neighbors, Joy was blessed both with intelligence and a gregarious personality.

While her family was not religious, it was Joy who persuaded her cousin, Susan Drew, to join her at Bible Camp at a Baptist church, and it was Joy who lured Susan into becoming a fellow Rainbow Girl, an Eastern Star Association for high school girls. As a young girl, she also was a member of the Junior Grange.

"She was very outgoing," Susan said. "Just a normal person."

From early childhood, Joy longed to teach English. In 1954, after graduating from Piscataquis Community High School, she moved to Orono, where she became a member of the University of Maine's class of 1958.

Though university life was surely a vast change from the country in Sangerville, the Orono community in the late 1950's was, for the most part, uncomplicated.

Old yearbooks from Joy's days at the University of Maine include scores of photographs of young men and women preparing for adulthood with closely monitored dances, zany parades through campus, late nights talking over sodas, and ash trays full of Lucky Strikes.

Although not one to draw attention to herself, Joy was a loyal friend, someone who might help others with their studies, who would pick up around the sorority room when no one else would, former sorority sisters at Delta Zeta recalled.

Joy's photograph for her junior year shows an attractive young woman with a round face, jet-black hair and a wistful smile.

A picture taken near the time of her death shows a pinched, bewildered face framed by bleached blonde hair and large glasses.

"She was a very pretty, happy, friendly person," said former sorority sister, Jessie Boivin. During her four years at Orono, Joy lived at the Elms, an old Victorian house located on the banks of the Stillwater River. A motel owned by the university stands there now.

She and the other fifty or so women who lived there spent their time playing bridge, going to dances and fraternity parties, working summer jobs, and studying late at night at the school library, Joy's former roommate, Cynthia Allen of Jefferson said.

Particularly close to her brother, Barry, who also was a student then, Joy enjoyed reading Chaucer and Hemingway.

After graduating in 1958 with a degree in English, Joy headed for her first teaching post, in Johnstown, New York, where for a year, she taught high school English and civics.

Like so many others who knew Joy over the years, most of her childhood and college friends did not keep in touch as she moved on to other chapters in her life.

"She sort of just really pulled away from all of us here," said Barbara Wilson, a former neighbor in Sangerville.

While home from college during one Christmas break, Joy met Drummond Easley, Jr., a soldier in the Army who was on his way to Korea.

Like Joy, "Bud," as he was known to his friends, came from a well-known family in the area. His father owned a local car dealership. During the next year or so, Joy finished her studies and spent the year teaching in New York,, while Bud completed his Army duty. They kept in touch through frequent letters.

And then, among baskets of snapdragons and daisies, Joy and Bud were married in June of 1960, during a large festive ceremony at the Methodist Church in nearby Dover-Foxcroft.

"She was an extremely sharp girl," said Malcolm Dow who served as best man at the wedding.

After settling down in Dover-Foxcroft, their first child, Drummond III was born in March of 1961. A second son, Scott, followed in April of 1963.

The fall after Drummond III was born, Joy taught college preparatory grammar to freshman at Piscataquis Community High School. She was a knowledgeable, straighforward teacher who did not put up with much from her fourteen year old students, said Gilbert Reynolds, now superintendent of schools in Greenville.

"She was a no-nonsense kind of person," Reynolds said. "You worked. She had high expectations for you."

"She was a nice person, she was a good teacher," said Edward

Hackett, the retired principal of the high school where Joy taught. He also was the one who hired her.

The pay at Piscataquis Community High School was low and the workload heavy. Joy moved on to Foxcroft Academy the next year, a position she left when she became pregnant with Scott.

Bud, meanwhile, worked at McDonald Ford Sales in Dover-Foxcroft, eventually rising to sales manager.

For the most part, the couple pretty much kept to themselves, although they would occasionally socialize with Dow.

"She was kind of a loner," said Matthew Williams, an old friend of the Easley famly. "But he was kind of a loner, too."

Friends and relatives say Joy began to show signs of mental illness, including paranoia, early in the marriage. It was the same illness that plagued an older brother, Evans, a former University of Massachusetts entomology professor who died last April. For both Joy and Evans, the illness would eventually consume their gifts.

Although the dates are uncertain, Joy would occasionally receive treatment at the Bangor Mental Health Institute. It was Williams, a justice of the peace, who first signed the papers to send her there.

"Unless you live with someone like that, it is very hard to understand," Bud said, adding that the mentally ill can typically function quite normally if they take their medication. "They can be more normal than you."

In July of 1967, Joy and Bud were divorced after seven years of marriage. That same year, he landed a job as the sales manager of Pine State Volkswagen in Bangor.

After the divorce, Joy spent a short time as a social worker, but left the job after an elderly patient committed suicide. She and Bud reconciled, and were married again in November of 1968, by a notary public in Sangerville.

In 1970, tired of commuting from Dover-Foxcroft to Bangor, Bud moved his family to an old farmhouse in Hudson, just outside Bangor. Joy's brief teaching career was over by the time they moved and she concentrated on raising their young sons.

Although they still did not socialize much in Hudson, there were trail bikes and snowmobiles for the boys, and Joy spent much of her time ferrying the children to ball games, Bud said.

As adults, the boys would discover success. Drummond III earned a doctorate and now works for the U.S. Bureau of Mines in Minnesota, while Scott, with a master's degree, is a biochemist in Montana.

In the mid-1980's, Joy was not taking her medication, and she took off, this time traveling around the western states until she had exhausted her share of money from the sale of some property.

In August of 1984, she was committed to the state hospital in Bangor for three months. Three months after that, she and Bud divorced again.

As she passed on to another stage in her life, Joy took a new name to accompany a fresh identity. It was part of the divorce decree that she changed her name to Alex James.

No one apparently knows the origin of this new identity, and during the times that she came home to visit her mother, everyone still called her Joy.

In the fall of 1985, the State Department of Human Services was on the brink of gaining court-ordered guardianship of Joy because she was not taking her medicine. After she promised to take the drugs, the Human Services department backed off.

For Bud, Alex James was a completely separate person that Joy Crafts, the young coed he had courted twenty-five years before.

"I have no regrets about what I did with my wife," he said, talking about differences between Joy Easley and Alex James. "But that woman was not my wife."

Toward the end of her life, Joy led an increasingly limited existence.

Because of her health problems, she rarely worked, could not drive a car, and relied on public assistance for income. Occasionally, one of her sons or brothers would check in on her.

Every so often, Bud would see her around town. But fearing that she might dredge up the old problems, he never stopped to talk.

In February of 1992, Joy received another blow. She was left temporarily homeless when her apartment house in Brewer burned down after another tenant's linseed oil-soaked rags spontaneously ignited. All four tenants escaped with only the clothes on their backs.

Joy started from scratch again and moved into another apartment just up the road. Former neighbors at both apartments described Joy as unfailingly polite, yet often withdrawn or nervous. Even those who knew her superficially said they could sometimes tell when she was not taking her medication.

Neighbors, acquaintances, and even landlords would offer her a ride when they saw her waiting for the city bus, but she never accepted.

Often, said former neighbor Jose Soares, Joy would leave the lights on in her apartment all night, then would set out for her walking errands early in the morning. "I don't know where she went," said Junior Fish, another former neighbor. "She was gone all day."

Usually Joy's day would begin with a walk up South Main Street to Tozier's Market or the Big Apple, where she would use food stamps to buy coffee and perhaps a doughnut. If she had enough change she would buy a pack of generic cigarettes and a newspaper. Cheryl York, a clerk at the Big Apple, remembered her as a "sweet, a very kind lady."

The closest Joy had to a friend during the more than three years she spent on South Main Street was Gertrude Ingalls, an elderly woman who would offer Joy a slice of pie and try to engage her in conversation. But even Ingalls, who considered Joy a good neighbor, knew little about her life history.

In Joy's apartment, there were no pets, no curtains on the windows, no old friends who visited, no music that drifted through the floor to the apartment below. The few people who actually saw the inside of her apartment found no traces of the books she had loved as a young woman.

Besides Ingalls, about the only consistent social life Joy had late in her life was the bus trip to the Brewer Shopping Center, which she would make two or three times a week.

It was here that she would wait for Shop 'n Save to open at seven a.m., so she could pick up a few groceries. She would then wait for the Brewer Laundromat to open half an hour later.

As her clothes were being washed, Joy would spend the next hour or so enjoying a cup of coffee, some cigarettes, and perhaps a few snippets of conversation with the morning attendant, Wendy Rose. The conversation with Rose was small talk only, concerning mundane but polite topics, such as the weather. Often Rose would ask Joy how she was doing, maybe whether she would be with family for Thanksgiving or Christmas.

Rose knew little of Joy's background, although she recalls that Joy once mentioned a brief stint as a chambermaid at a local motel.

On Friday, June 16, Joy dressed in clothes familiar to those who knew her, blue-and-white striped slacks, a black shirt, white sneakers and a green nylon windbreaker. As always, she was carrying a multi-colored bag she used as a purse.

As she waiting for her laundry that morning, Joy gave Rose three small pieces of candy as they chatted and drank coffee. Her clothes ready, she walked back up the plaza to catch the bus near the supermarket.

That afternoon, at about four thirty, Joy's neighbors watched her walk out of her apartment. The last confirmed sighting of her was around six p.m. at the Bangor Mall.

And then, at six forty-five a.m., Saturday, a man who rented a building at the industrial park found her body, nude and beaten, her throat slashed. She was lying in a patch of grass ten feet from the road.

Police have said the murder was random, that Joy apparently was picked up as she went about one of her walks, and in all probability, it was the first time in years that Joy, who had changed from an outgoing country girl to a woman whose illness had made her so cautious, had been in a car.

It was Pure Fright. I Became so Scared.

Amanda Carr was thirteen years old when waves of panic and terror hit her with such stunning force she believed she was dying.

"It was pure fright. I became so scared. I was having hot and cold flashes, numbness," said the sixteen year old.

She ran to the nurse's office, shaking all over, her speech muted.

She did manage to tell the nurse to call her mother.

Nancy Carr remembers the call. "I said, 'Who is that screaming in the background?'"

"Your daughter," the nurse replied.

Amanda's mother ran six blocks to the school, and tried to calm Amanda, who kept screaming that she wanted to go to a hospital. Instead, she was taken home, where she stayed for three months, refusing to go to school, mostly lying in bed. She would not let her mother out of her sight, and often woke up screaming at night, insisting upon getting into bed with her mother.

David Carr, Amanda's father, spent most of his nights on the couch. Amanda lost weight and refused to take telephone calls from her friends. Eventually most of them stopped calling.

Nancy Carr began a cycle many parents of children with mental illness adopt. She tried every day to get her daughter up for school, thinking this would be the morning when Amanda would get up, dress and go off to class just like she had before.

Instead, there were roaring temper tantrums on Amanda's part as her mother alternately tried being sweet, angry or tearful in her attempt to get her daughter to school.

Schools are not particularly sympathetic to undiagnosed mental illness. Instead, they pay more attention to attendance, conformity and the school's image.

Amanda's school in Lewiston began calling frequently, asking what was wrong and when she would return. The family doctor said there was nothing wrong with the girl, that she was simply a spoiled child having a copy-cat illness because her dying grandfather was taking up a great deal of her mother's time.

"I was there for my dad, for my grandmother in the nursing home, for my daughter," said Nancy, fighting back tears. It was her duty, she thought, to make her daughter well.

During this time, the Carrs ran head on into one of the major smears in the treatment of mental illness, the lack of services for children and adolescents. In Maine, only thirteen psychiatrists work exclusively with that age group, more than there were five years ago, but still not enough.

The State Bureau of Children with Special Needs in its 1993-1994 report, said only about one-quarter of the needs of young people between the ages of six and nineteen are being met. The cost of neglect is enormous, as much as forty-two million dollars a year. That is because youg people with mental illness are more likely to drop out of school, wind up in the correctional system, or require treatment for substance abuse.

Children also are placed into expensive special education classes without a diagnosis. And parents lose time from work caring for them.

As recently as five years ago, just before Amanda became ill, there was no network of services for young people in Maine, despite at least ten thousand children identified with severe emotional problems or mental illness.

Augusta Mental Health Institute has closed its adolescent unit. Kennebec Valley Medical Center in Augusta has no psychiatric beds for adolescents, and neither do most private hospitals. There are two in Maine that take children, Jackson Brooke in Portland and Arcadia in Bangor.

The Carrs finally found a program in Lewiston, run by St. Mary's Regional Medical Center. But getting there was not easy.

"I called about six psychiatrists," Nancy said. Some could not see Amanda right away, others did not treat thirteen year olds, and others would not take her because she was on Medicaid at that time.

In the meantime, a tutor was lined up to come to Amanda's house to help her keep up with homework. The arrangement failed but Nancy Carr went to school every day, to pick up her daughter's homework.

Some mornings she was able to pull her daughter out of bed and the mother and daughter would go to school, Amanda with uncombed hair and an unwashed face, Nancy pushing her every step of the way.

Amanda stayed in school only if her mother stayed, too, right beside her in a chair. The longest the girl stayed was for one class. One day the mother was sitting in the back of the room.

"Amanda turned around and her face went white. She said, 'Mama.' Her lips were quivering, she was very white, and everywhere I touched her, I could feel a heartbeat," the mother said.

They left the school. The same day, Nancy called Youth in Transition, a program at St. Mary's that treats adolescents just out of the hospital or those who cannot cope with the outside world.

There, a doctor diagnosed Amanda as having panic disorder. He also said she was not well enough to be in school, and started her on medication.

Reluctantly, Amanda began going to the youth center three years ago. She eventually spent up to five hours a day there, receiving group and individual therapy. She was tutored at home and finished eighth grade at the dining room table.

The anti-depressant and anti-anxiety medication she took began to ease the panic attacks.

"Until we got here, it was hell," Nancy said as the whole family sat in the Youth in Transition office. "It is very frustrating." The whole family suffered, she said. There was tension, fighting, screaming and tears as each family member tried to do something for Amanda, often disagreeing on what should be done.

Linda Horn, manager of Youth in Transition, remembers clearly the first time she met Amanda. "She was thin and white, and had tears running down her face because she didn't want her mother to leave her," Horn said.

She sees a lot of young people like that in the program that serves twelve adolescents between the ages of thirteen and seventeen. The program is structured to keep young people with mental illness out of the hospital and help them take the steps back into society.

Its cost is about one-third what it costs to keep a young person hospitalized. Most young people who enter the program stay anywhere from three to six months, although some stay as long as a year.

"Morning is school time," Horn said. The teens either attend regular schools or go to the Sweetser School in Lewiston.

The program serves a broad area around Lewiston, usually those within a thirty mile radius. Participants must provide their own transportation. The young people arrive during the late morning, after a partial day of school, then have lunch at a cafeteria nearby.

After lunch, there are two group sessions. One to help the teens gain insight into themselves, the other to help them learn about their illnesses and how to cope with them.

The young people can leave the building for appointments with their therapists. Family therapy is held once a week.

"This was started as a resource for adolescents," Horn said. The only other such program is in Bangor.

Near Youth in Transition is Genesis House, a group home for adolescent boys run by the Department of Human Services. To get into the program, the boys must be in state custody.

"Most cannot go home, for any number of reasons," said program manager Paula Mortensen. "They have problems that started a long time ago." The home holds up to eight boys who have been hospitalized.

"There are not enough services for mentally ill kids," Mortensen said. "Not enough. I cannot emphasize that enough." Sometimes expensive hospitalization is prolonged because there is no place to house state wards coming out of St. Mary's. Much more housing is needed for that population.

Until very recently, parents often were encouraged to give up custody of their children to the state, so the children would receive unrestricted treatment. Doctors would actually suggest that parents do this. But in 1994, the Legislature passed a law saying children could live at home and receive the state services.

Boys can stay at Genesis for up to eighteen months, in a home-like setting that has firm rules and a system of privileges based on points for good behavior. The points can be used for any number of things from a walk outside at the beginning, to a trip to the mall on Friday night.

Genesis House is unlocked and the stay is voluntary. Each boy has an individualized plan for the future, and the residents are free to take jobs, date and participate in activities at the local high school.

"There's a lot more awareness about mental illness now," Mortensen said. "It's not as shameful anymore." The most common illnesses of the young people at the home are attention deficit disorder, which carries with it behavior problems, and mood disorders such as depression and manic depression.

The house is near the hospital and has a medical director. If problems arise, both facilities and a doctor are nearby. There is also at the home daily group therapy, household chores and an evening study period.

"We offer structure, treatment and help with everyday living," Mortensen said.

As for Amanda Carr, she is now a rosy-cheeked teenager with dark hair and a ready smile. She has gained back most of her weight.

And she cannot remember the last time she had a panic attack.

Would You Feel This Way About My Son if He Had Cancer?

Joyce Roy cringed every time the telephone rang.

Invariably it was someone calling to discuss her son, Benjamin. He had caused trouble on the playground again. He had gone to a birthday party and badly spoiled the fun. Or he had stolen something and denied taking it.

At home he punched holes in the wall, hacked the furniture, trashed his bedroom, and hid spoiling bags of food around the house.

"It seems like his problems were coming so fast that we couldn't help him. We wanted him to get through the knothole, but the knothole was getting smaller and he was coming too fast," said Ben's father, Norman Roy.

Ben, now thirteen, remembers how his emotions would overpower him. "I was confused. And I sort of had trouble making decisions. And I'd get mad at the littlest thing. I'd blow up in Mom or Dad's face, they'd send me to my room and I'd trash the room. Later, I would apologize."

Ben was adopted when he was two years old. His mother noticed he was unusually combative and angry for a child of that age. "Even when he was four, the babysitter had questions about his anger," Joyce recalled.

By kindergarten, there were real problems. "The first time he rode the bus was a disaster," his mother said. "He couldn't handle the stimulation. They were threatening to kick him off."

Calls came from the school at least once a week, then more frequently as Ben became older. If he had friends over, he would become overexcited and the friends would leave. If he went to a friend's house, he often was not invited back. "And he was always segregated at school, always seated near the teacher," Joyce said.

The parents, meanwhile, found melted ice cream in the bureau drawers and rotting fruit stashed behind a couch. "I liked hiding things. Period," Ben said. He also stole money, toys, pencils from the other kids, and his father's tools.

"I'd find my tools out in the woods somewhere," Norman said. Ben did not consider what he did as stealing. "Those things were cool. I wanted them."

In first grade, he was nearly expelled for calling the teacher dirty names. And his parents became more and more desperate.

Norman dreaded coming home from his job at Digital Equipment Corp., for he knew he would have to hear about what Ben had done that day. Joyce, who worked for the state until the family problems forced a leave of absence, became more and more emotionally exhausted.

Tensions within the family mounted. Everyone walked on egg shells.

Each parent withheld things about Ben from the other, Joyce because she could not listen to her husband lose his temper one more time, and Norman, because he did not want to put more strain on his wife.

"We fought. We grew apart instead of closer," Norman said. That is a common side effect of having a mentally ill family member, especially when it is a child. There are quarrels about the proper treatment, how much should be expected of the sick person, and sometimes, whether the family member is really mentally ill, or just lazy. The divorce rate among parents of mentally ill children is quite high, often because the father cannot accept the illness. One woman who is now active with the Alliance for the Mentally Ill of Maine became divorced after her son developed Schizophrenia.

The father, a psychologist, could not stand having a son like that and blamed the boy's illness on the mother, instead of acknowledging that the sickness was a chemical imbalance of the brain.

With the Roys, Norman would become so upset he would shout. That only made things worse, he said.

"Ben could be helpful and sweet, but we never knew when he was going to pop. It might have been every other day, but it seemed like every day," Joyce said. "It was like, when will this ever end?"

As the parents grew apart, they also blamed themselves for Ben's behavior, thinking maybe they were the wrong adoptive parents for him.

He was placed in counseling when he was in kindergarten, and, after a long discussion with a pediatrician, the boy was put on Ritalin, a drug intended to calm hyperactive behavior and anger. "It helped for awhile, but then it just didn't do me any good," Ben said. His counselor thought Ben was hyperactive, but Joyce did not think so. His attention span was good, and he had no trouble concentrating.

But that still left the question of what was wrong.

"Sometimes I would feel so bad," Ben said. He spent many nights crying, wondering why he behaved as he did, why he was always being reprimanded at school.

When he was in second grade, Ben began seeing a child psychiatrist in Lewiston. He was put on an anti-depressant and joined a group therapy session. Every week for two years, Joyce and Norman took turns leaving work early to drive Ben to therapy.

It did not seem to be working.

Norman, who used to stay in the waiting room during the hour long session, was called in three times to calm his son down, because the therapist could not do anything with Ben.

"Here's a psychiatrist and he couldn't control the group. Ben was that disruptive," Norman said. Usual procedures such as time outs, asking Ben to apologize, or talking to him alone, did not have any impact.

By now, Ben's behavior was taking on serious proportions. He climbed out on the roof at school, the fights on the playground became more violent, he held a match to the ceiling at home and pricked pinholes in his parents' waterbed.

When Joyce was at work, she would receive calls about him and burst into tears. Norman had trouble concentrating at his job. The school, in general, cooperated. Ben was in special education classes and school officials kept trying different plans to improve his behavior.

The plans would work for two or three days, the parents would get their hopes up, then everything would fall apart again. There would be more destruction, more telephone calls.

Neither the medication nor the therapy was helping.

The Roy's private insurance covered half their son's visits to the doctor, but the other half came from their own pockets. Their share came to thousands of dollars each year.

Insurance companies discriminate when it comes to treatment for mental illness, by putting limits on benefits. Until a few years ago, the lifetime cap for mental illness treatment in Maine was twenty-five thousand dollars. One brief hospital stay can wipe that out.

Psychiatrists are reimbursed fifty percent by insurance companies and hospital days per year are limited to sixty.

But Maine, this year, became only the third state in the country to achieve full coverage for mental illness. The state Legislature, over the objections of the insurance lobby, voted for parity for severe mental disorders, allowing the same coverage as for physical illnesses. The lifetime cap will be lifted on January 1, 1996 and other benefits will rise as well. The only other states with full equality are Rhode Island and New Hampshire.

Families have gone broke in the past trying to help their mentally ill children by taking out second mortgages, using up all their savings, or selling their houses so family members can continue treatment.

The danger now is that managed care plans are going to destroy psychiatry, by still limiting the treatment in an effort to hold down costs.

"Try telling someone just out of the hospital that he is entitled to just six aftercare visits to a psychiatrist," one doctor said.

Ben Roy was not getting any better, despite the mounting costs. "Things were really, really bad," Joyce said.

She took the leave of absence from work because she did not dare leave Ben alone for any length of time. The family also became isolated as it wrestled with a problem so large that there seemed to be no solution. Relatives who did not understand what the family was going through said Ben was simply a brat who needed to be spanked once in a while.

Eventually Ben lost interest in school, throwing his homework out the window of the bus on the way home each day. His father would go back later and try to find it. "I'd say, 'Now, where do you think you threw it? Right along here?' and I'd look in the ditches and along the side of the road," Norman said.

Two years ago, upon the advice of the psychiatrist, Ben was taken to Jackson Brook Institute in Portland. There, he was given a complete physical workup and evaluated by a team of doctors.

He was hospitalized for two months and finally diagnosed with post traumatic stress disorder (from abuse before he was adopted), attention deficit disorder, and emerging manic depression. The doctors began a course of lithium. Ben went to classes at the hospital and began living in the kind of firm environment that children with behavioral disorders require.

"I felt safer at the hospital," said Ben, who admitted he did not always feel safe at school.

Two years ago, after much discussion with the Winthrop School System, the child was placed in the residential Sweetser Home and School in Saco, at the Winthrop school department's expense.

School systems do not like placing students in such places for a number of reasons, cost being the major one. It costs about thirty-two thousand dollars to place someone like Ben in a residential school for one year. The cost can be more than one hundred thousand dollars if the placement has to be out-of-state.

When a student leaves a school, the school system also loses the state subsidy on that pupil, about four thousand six hundred dollars on average in Maine.

And, no school wants to admit that it can not help a student. That is saying that the school has failed, and that the teachers fell down on their jobs.

"Winthrop kept insisting that they could develop a program for Ben, and I kept insisting that they couldn't," Joyce said. "They hadn't been able to control him in the past, and he was getting worse."

At the home in Saco, Ben lived a normal life, going to school, working on his behavior and coming home every other weekend. On the alternate weekends, his parents went to see him. They had to choose careful activities to avoid over-stimulating him.

At the end of the past school year, he was allowed to come home for a trial period and to go to school back in Winthrop.

His parents are keeping their fingers crossed. Having a child with a mental illness is a sensitive issue for the whole family. "Mental illness, there's some kind of shame involved," Joyce said. "Stigma. You don't like to tell people about it."

But then she said, "Ben is a boy with a mental illness. He has a chemical imbalance and he can't control the things he does. He's judged by other people as being bad. But he's spent many nights crying and wanting to die, because he knows what he does is wrong, but he can't help it."

"Would you feel this way about my son if he had diabetes or cancer?"

I Thought the Hospital Was the White House

When Richard Wilcox developed schizophrenia, he first thought he was Jesus Christ.

And he was dating a mentally ill girl who thought she was the Virgin Mary. "We used to sit around and read the Bible a lot and talk about how we were saving the universe," said Wilcox, twenty-six, who lives in a boarding home in Portland.

While it was pleasing going around blessing people and forgiving their sins, Wilcox was happier when be became President of the United States.

"My writings at school and my talking became irrational. I'd write these memos saying, 'I see, Mr. President,' or I'd tell people how I wanted things done," he said.

As he talks, Richard sometimes looks away, avoiding eye contact, another trait of his illness. He also shifts in his chair and seems a little agitated.

"I'm sorry, I sometimes get a little nervous."

He was with the Job Corps program in Bangor when he first became ill, although he says now it was just a matter of time before sickness would descend. It was the staff at Job Corps that first took him to the hospital, to Bangor Mental Health Institute.

"I thought it was pretty nice there, because I thought it was the White House," he said.

Richard ordered people around, gave requests for certain foods, wrote memos, and treated the place as if it were his own.

"Actually they were pretty good to me there," he said. But hospital officials decided Richard needed a more extensive evaluation, so he was sent to Jackson Brook Institute in Portland, a hospital that treats adolescents. Richard was eighteen at the time. At Jackson Brook, he received the diagnosis of schizophrenia with manic-depressive features.

He was in a fix. Schizophrenia is the most difficult of mental illnesses, because treatment until recently produced only marginal results.

Schizophrenia is a thought disorder, one that carries with it delusions, hallucinations, paranoia and complete breaks with reality. Those are the most obvious symptoms, and medications have been able to treat or lessen those for quite some time.

But the disease has a secondary set of symptoms that are more tricky, depression, withdrawal, anti-social behavior, difficulty making decisions and conversation, and lack of motivation. Those symptoms were not touched by older medications, and not until the advent of Clozaril about five years ago was there anything on the market for the whole spectrum of schizophrenia. Now there is an even newer drug, Risperdol.

Manic depression, or bipolar illness, as it is usually called, is a mood disorder, characterized by highs and lows, mood changes so extreme that the person can go from euphoria to despair in the course of a single day.

Richard went to Jackson Brook in 1987, where he spent three weeks in therapy and was put on medication. Since then, he has been hospitalized fifteen more times, and more than once in every psychiatric unit in central and southern Maine. He spent eighteen months at the Augusta Mental Health Institute, where, he said, "I was locked up for fighting, and they just filled me full of meds."

He has also spent time on the psychiatric ward at Maine Medical Center and at a hospital in Brunswick. "I'd get sick. I'd get delusional again, and I'd be taken off to the hospital," he said of the cycle.

The delusions and other symptons would come because he would go off his medications, something that the mentally ill do all the time.

"You think you're getting better, that you don't need them anymore," Richard said. For a short time, the patient feels fine, then the depressions or hallucinations or highs began filtering in, eventually smothering the person. By that time, it is too late to handle the crisis alone.

Some patients go off medications because of the side effects, such as sleepiness, or insomnia, bowel disorders, dry mouth, rapid heartbeat, or trembling hands.

And others refuse to take medications simply because they cannot acknowledge that they have a mental illness, an illness that robs vitality and reason, one that carries the greatest of stigma of any illness within society.

Richard knew when he was eight years old that something was wrong with him. His mother ran out on the family and he was brought up by foster parents. He later went to live with his father in Portland, and stayed one year. "My father was abusive. I didn't know what I was getting into," he says now.

He also lived with a series of aunts, with a cousin, and finally with a foster family in Gray.

"I had happy moments," he said of his childhood. Yet when he was five and in kindergarten, he exhibited behavioral problems. He pushed his teacher out of her chair, he ran away from home a couple of times, into the woods, where he would be found a day or two later. He also had violent fits of crying.

When he was about eight, his foster parents said something had to be done about all the stuffed animals Richard owned. He took everyone of them outside and burned them. "I had to get rid of them."

His grades were always just average, because his mind wandered all the time. Like most children with problems, but with undiagnosed mental illness, he was placed in special education.

By the time he reached his teens, Richard was using drugs and alcohol to dull his pain. "Emotionally, I was a nervous wreck. I was paranoid. I was afraid people were after me. I hated middle school."

But in high school he was popular and athletic, running track and cross-country. And he wrote well, so well that his teachers commented on it and suggested he do something with his talent.

After graduation, he was placed in Job Corps, a program designed to help underachievers learn a trade. He was at the Bangor center only a month before he snapped.

"And that's what I did. I just snapped. I wouldn't talk. I memorized all the materials for my certified nurse's assistant class, but today, I can't remember one thing I learned," he said.

His writings and speech became more and more incoherent, until he was taken to the hospital.

Richard today lives in a boarding home run by Shalom House, Inc., in Portland. The non-profit organization runs a series of group homes, boarding homes, apartments, community services and other housing needs for the mentally ill.

There are three group homes, three rooming houses, twelve subsidized apartments and thirty-one apartments funded through the state and federal governments.

That sounds like a lot of housing, but the boarding homes and group residences have very small populations, anywhere from six to fifteen people. The corporation serves one hundred sixty clients and has a staff of forty case managers, support workers, group home administrators and central office staff.

That sounds like a great many people, but as Joseph Brannigan, executive director of Shalom House, said, "Some of the care is very intensive. We have one person who needs a team of seven people around the clock." That means someone must be with that person at all times.

It is not unusual in talking to the mentally ill to find that one person alone has a case worker, two or three staff supporters, a therapist, a counselor and a job coach. Still, the cost is much less than keeping the mentally ill person in the hospital. A number of support workers make no more than ten thousand dollars a year. The same kind of worker at Augusta Mental Health Institute would make twice that, which is one reason hospitalization is so expensive.

The Shalom House Corporation has divided its housing units into those for the most functional former patients and those with the fewest skills. Some people live almost entirely on their own, seeing their case manager once a week. Others need help with living skills, conflict resolution and other methods of coping with life outside the hospital. The group and boarding homes have live-in staff who spend the night. Residents are encouraged to leave the houses in the morning for job training or to work.

Former patients may move from one kind of housing to another as they recover from their illnesses. Shalom House itself, the name of one of the residences, can serve as an example.

Patients can stay there for eighteen months, where the first nine months focus on gaining independent living skills, such as shopping, taking medications on time and making friends. There are twelve beds in the home. The program is informal and each resident is encouraged to structure his or her own life in a way that promotes growth and mental health.

The last three months of the program emphasize finding permanent housing and community support.

Just as people can move up the ladder of the housing units, they also can go back to the half-way house or to a more protected environment, if necessary.

Shalom House is located in downtown Portland, where former patients can walk or take city transport to medical and other resources. Very few people with mental illness drive, mainly because they cannot afford car payments or because their illness struck just at the age when they would be earning licenses.

Even in the most informal settings within the Shalom House program, residents are expected to do chores, take turns cooking and attend weekly group meetings.

Shalom House, Inc., is the largest facility of its kind in Maine, yet it does not begin to fill the need for housing for the mentally ill. Just recently, a group of clients of the mental health system held a rally in Portland complaining of lack of housing and the cost when housing can be found.

Protesters said seventy-five percent of the beds taken up in the city's homeless shelters are occupied by people with mental illness, people who overstay the thirty-day limit because they have no where to go. Some are physically sick as well as mentally ill, others are single mothers with small children.

People who run homeless shelters are not always trained to deal with the mentally ill, so there are disturbances, and sometimes the person is asked to leave.

The Shalom House program is for patients who have been hospitalized, usually at the Augusta Mental Health Institute, which services the Portland area.

Richard lives in Vaughan Street House, a boarding home for six people, permanent housing for patients recovering from illnesses. There are individual support staff who can assist with living skills, but residents must be capable of taking some care of themselves. The home is not designed for upsetting or disruptive behavior. The house has a building manager, a weekly meeting and the sharing of household chores.

Each person has a private room with a bed, dresser and small refrigerator. Residents are free to bring their own furniture. The kitchen, dining room, living room and two bathrooms are shared. The rental cost is thirty percent of the person's income, which usually comes from disability checks or a combination of disability and a minimum wage job. There would be no way that anyone living on disability could afford the regular rents in Portland, which are well over one thousand dollars a month.

Richard's home is supported by the state, Medicaid and a federal grant. That same kind of mixture supports all the housing, thus keeping the rents at a reasonable level for the resident.

Richard describes his life this way: "Get up in the morning, take our meds, go to work, come home and eat supper, watch some TV, go to bed, and get up the next day and do it all over again."

Two different residents share the cooking each night. Richard right now works preparing meals for pre-school programs. He actually washes dishes and cleans around the kitchen, he confesses. He works up to twelve hours a week and makes $4.65 an hour. If he makes too much, he will lose his disability.

"You don't have to work," he said of where he lives. "You can come and go as you please. But most people leave the house during the day."

With six people, there are misunderstandings, he said, but that is what the house manager and the weekly meetings are for.

Richard has a case worker who he sees once a week, a job coach, a social club to go to that is run by the Alliance for Mentally Ill of Maine, two doctors (a psychiatrist and a psychologist), and friends at the home.

Some may wonder why he needs two doctors. That is the preferred treatment for people as seriously ill as Richard. The psychiatrist takes care of the medications, and the psychologist, who is not allowed to prescribe drugs, takes care of the talking therapy. The talking can be just as beneficial as the pills, sometimes more so. The usual course of treatment given to a person released from the hospital is take your meds, see your therapist regularly, try to establish a routine, and do not push things too fast. And, oh yes, it helps to eat well, too.

Richard pays one hundred eighty-three dollars in rent from his disability check and receives ten dollars a month in food stamps. He makes too much money to qualify for more. Medicaid takes care of treatment.

There are some drawbacks to being on Medicaid. It took Shalom House officials a couple of months to find a dentist who would take Medicaid patients. Richard also walks everywhere, and his house is a mile from the center of downtown. On the other hand, he is close to Maine Medical Center, the doctor's office for the mentally ill, where he goes for emergency treatment.

I Can't Get Mad, I Can't Have a Good Cry

When William Hazlett's brain skyrockets into mania, his mind and mouth take off like a machine gun.

"The high becomes like a roller coaster ride," he said, imitating the motion of the amusement park ride with his hand. "Then it begins going faster and faster," he said, moving his hand more swiftly.

At those times he can consume everything going around him and in the outside world, he said. "It's like, want to talk about medication advances in the Twentieth Century? Sure. Want to talk about prehistoric skeletal remains? Fine. And what about how Clinton is handling that thing over in Bosnia? That's interesting, too," he said. And so it goes as his mind expands to the point that he thinks he knows the answers to the universe.

"When I'm like that, I know the answers to almost everything. I have a thousand opinions, and I can draw them out on blueprints," he said.

Hazlett is a talkative man even when he is not going through mania. His insights are stunning and he has an edge of brilliance about him.

He plays in a band called "Misty Haze," a band formed for the mentally ill in the Bangor area. He taught himself to play harmonica and electric guitar, and his tastes in music are eclectic: B.B. King, Tom T. Hall, Hank Williams, Sr., the Statler Brothers, Patsy Cline.

There is one he adores, one some people have never heard of: Nana Mouskouri, the Greek singer. "She sings angelic songs. When I hear her, my heart just rises. I can get so high just listening to her," he said.

He remembers some of the old-timers who used to play on Stacey's Jamboree, a local show broadcast in the 1960's from a restaurant in Bangor. Some of the talent was good, some was not. Especially when the show allowed anyone who wished to come on. It was televised late at night over a Bangor television station.

Along with picking up music on his own, Hazlett is a self-taught artist. He shows some of his drawings, which are overwhelmingly complicated, so detailed that the viewer is perplexed.

It was those drawings that first tipped people off that Hazlett might suffer from mania. He was in high school doing extraordinarily precise art that included hundreds of objects and shapes.

"When I'd try to explain them to people, they'd say they were too detailed," he said. It was as if he had to encompass everything into his art. And he had the memory for it. "If I saw a helicopter, I could remember exactly what it looked like and I'd put it into the picture."

As a young man, he was thought of as merely energetic. As he got older, it became apparent that it was something more than that.

He had his first breakdown a month before he graduated from Bangor High School.

"I came from a large, loving family. I was the oldest of ten kids. I suppose that didn't help matters. But my mother was on welfare and I wanted to help out. I went to school in the morning, then did work-study in the afternoon. After that I held down two part-time jobs after school. I wouldn't get home at night until eleven o'clock or so. It was too much."

Even before his breakdown, there were flashy acts, grandiose thinking. "Do you know what my first car was? Most kids get a second-hand jalopy. Mine was a gold Cadillac. I worked for it, and I paid four hundred dollars for it."

His episode of exhaustion and mania was called a nervous breakdown, the name given to all psychiatric disorders in the 1950's and 1960's. Everyone who went to the state hospital had "nervous problems" or "an emotional upset." Nobody was mentally ill.

Part of that was because doctors could not be as precise in their diagnosis as they are today (although everyone today seems to be labeled as bipolar). The other problem was the lack of medications.

When Hazlett went to the hospital, he was shot full of Thorazine. "It was unbelievable. I'd sit there saying, 'I'm expanding my mind,' and I couldn't even reach my plastic fork to get to my dinner plate."

He received his diploma from Bangor High School despite not being able to take part in graduation.

He next went to Beal College, a small business and trade school, to take a two-year course to become a veterinarian's assistant. His plan was to go out-of-state and finish the training required to become a veterinarian.

"But the strings were pulled back on college loans. This was during the Nixon years. So that cut me right out," he said. "I went into construction. The union paid for me to go to school to learn how to set up a laser beam light. Now, that was right up my alley, because I can draw Star Wars pictures and pictures of the galaxies. I loved that. Do you know if you put a laser light the wrong way, you can blind a guy? It's very precise work."

Hazlett has a problem with hospitals and doctors making judgements about people being a danger to themselves or others as a criteria for admission.

"What's a danger to oneself? I used to work construction. I can walk out on a steel beam and not fall. I know how to do that. Am I a danger to myself? What might be a danger to one person is not a danger to someone else," he said.

Actually, doctors use the definition in terms of suicide or homicide attempts, and many people have learned that if they want to go into the hospital to get away from it all, or if they want to stay longer, all they have to say is that they are having suicidal thoughts.

Unfortunately, teen-agers who are state wards often use that ploy rather than be sent to yet another foster home. The result is hospital stays that are longer than necessary for those adolescents.

Hazlett's hospital visits became more and more frequent after he reached adulthood. "I was in and out six or seven times. I've lost count."

"They didn't have the proper meds then. There was no counseling, nothing," he said. He was put in a strait jacket more than once and on one occasion got out of it and swung it in the air at the doctors, like Harry Houdini.

"I just felt like my mind was being picked all the time. My days were taken up by analytical sons of bitches who thought they knew me. They didn't know me, that I like to hunt and fish and swim, all those open space things. They didn't know that being confined in the hospital made me worse. When they look at the records, all they see is how many shots you'd had that day and how many pills. They never ask the patient a thing."

Hazlett was in seclusion more than once and at one point escaped from a locked ward. Mania gives people the impression of power, invincibility, and manic patients can be hard to handle because their strength increases tremendously when they are in an episode.

One fellow in Bangor told me about being so angry and hostile that it took twenty staffers to hold him down when he got to the hospital.

Police also fear people like Hazlett. "If someone calls the police and asks them to come to my house because I'm manic, I don't get just one cop, I get five," Hazlett said. The calls are usually made by his ex-wife who also is mentally ill, or by a neighbor.

To look at Hazlett, one might think he was a high school basketball coach. He has sandy, short-cropped hair, an outgoing nature, and a sense of leadership about him. He is the kind of man who probably could inspire a group of young people to go for the championship.

Instead, he goes to his camp when things get rough. "Stress and pressure set me of." Then he goes from being charming to becoming very irritable, smashing dishes and other objects in his house and talking in extremely loud tones.

"I get scared and run into the other room," his wife, Patsy, said. Now she's learned to say, "Get out of here. Go out to camp for two or three days." And he does. There, the lake, the quiet, the sound of the loons and the solitude of fishing soothe his roaring brain. "I love that place. As soon as I start driving down that camp road, I feel better."

His wife has three children from a former marriage. All three have some kind of mental disorder. Two of them have attention deficit and hyperactivity. The third has childhood depression.

Hazlett tries to spend as much time with them as he can, and has become very involved in their treatment. He often takes one or more of them with him to camp.

But a number of things bother Hazlett, because he is a man of moods. "I can't get mad, you see, like other people, or someone calls the cops on me. I can't sit in the corner and have a good cry, or someone will say, 'What's wrong? You sick? Manic depressive, huh?'"

"I feel like a yo-yo, but I'm not allowed to express my emotions," he said with some sarcasm.

This is a common problem of the mentally ill. If they have a night when they can not sleep, they and everyone else wonder if it is an episode of mania coming on. If the person has a down day, the fear is that a depressive episode is looming. The mentally ill person is supposed to stay on an even keel, otherwise, there will be questions about whether medications have been taken, whether the person is feeling all right, if it might be better to take a pill and lie down instead of going out for the evening.

Most people with mental illness grow to know themselves very well after awhile, by learning when a symptom is really a symptom and when it is not. In general, symptoms have to last for a matter of weeks, or at least days, before they require attention.

There are, of course, crises that last a day or two or three, acute episodes of suicidal thoughts or other discomfort. What is necessary in such cases are crisis beds, not hospitalization. And Maine does not have enough crisis beds. The bulk of them are between Bangor and Portland, and there are none in the eastern and northern sections of the state.

Hazlett has plenty to say about services in Bangor and in Maine in general.

"There are not enough services and not enough of the right kind," he said. "You go into a counseling center and there's some nineteen year old high school graduate who would rather be a model than a mental health worker. And she's asking you questions about whether your marriage is OK or whether the kids are getting on your nerves. She's never been married. She's never had kids. What does she know about any of that?"

He prefers organizations like peer support groups, whereby the mentally ill help each other through discussion. That was tried at the social club he belongs to, he said, but was closed down by the administration because the club members supposedly were finding out too much about each other.

"The administrators try to keep the lid on our independence, so they can keep their jobs," he said.

As an example, he told of how he and some other members of the mentally ill community in Bangor opened a restaurant, their own business.

"It was closed because the administration of the club cut back the pay and the hours. The state Bureau of Vocational Rehabilitation didn't like it. They said, 'Let's turn it into a job-training program and the hours can be from ten a.m. to three p.m.,'" Hazlett said. That way, the employees would be paid one dollar an hour.

"They said it was competing with another restaurant nearby," he continued. "Now you don't run a successful restaurant with hours like ten to three. You have to be open at six a.m., so people can come in and get some coffee and breakfast on the way to work. And you have to be open in the early evening, so they can get some supper," he said.

"We've been through so much of this stuff that we know it like the back of our hands," he said of attempts at independence. He also has some reservations about calling people in the mental health system "consumers." A consumer can pick and choose what he wants, the mentally ill cannot. They are strapped down by a system that thinks of employment as pushing trays in a cafeteria.

"Where are the cures for mental illness?" Hazlett asked. "Where are the cures? There are just a lot of silly questions and a lot of programs that do not work. They just keep the system going so to get more money. Maine gets millions of dollars each year for these programs. But these people create problems to keep programs going. If a program fails, that is a good excuse to ask for more money to make it work or to start a new program," he said.

When asked why the mentally ill do not organize and march on Augusta with their complaints, Hazlett and a friend laughed.

"People are afraid of us," the friend said. "Every year they take us to Augusta during Mental Illness Awareness Week, and we go down to Capitol Park and they parade us around."

"Then we go to the governor's mansion for a cup of tea, and the whole time we're there, the governor's staff is all nervous, afraid one of us is going to smash out a window."

The Only Thing I Had Was Being Down and Out

The Together Place in Bangor once was an Elks Club and before that, a morgue.

Today it is a social club for the mentally ill, a gathering place for coffee and food, cigarettes and conversation, television and newspapers. The organization also runs a crisis center with four beds, a hotline for emergencies, and supported employment for its employees.

In the early morning, someone is frying pancakes and making toast. The coffee comes in oversized cups. There is an air of friendliness, where members shake hands with visitors and welcome them. There is pride here, comradeship, love.

A club member sitting with a walkman on his head is asked what he is listening to. "Songs," he replies. The answer makes more sense than the question.

He later says he is listening to the Beatles. George Harrison is his favorite of the foursome. Does he remember when the group appeared on Ed Sullivan in 1965? No, he is too young for that.

Fifteen of Maine's counties have social clubs for the mentally ill, the one exception being Washington County.

The Bangor club is part of a network of services that includes a shelter for the homeless, at least one counseling center, and a state hospital for the mentally ill. There also is Eastern Maine Medical Center, a large modern facility that serves the needs of the eastern part of the state.

The Unitarian Church is just a few hundred yards from the Together Place, and club members sometimes go there for bean suppers. That church, they say, offers a welcoming heart to the city's mentally ill population.

While some club members say they have outgrown the Together Place and want to move on to more independence, others will spend the rest of their days there, listening to music, lost in their own fantasies.

The first thing one notices about the club is how members watch out for each other. Those who are most competent make sure the dignity of the less functional is protected. No one bothers the fellow sitting alone with the walkman. The more outgoing members sit at tables drinking coffee, smoking, and joshing each other. But if the joking or discussion gets out of hand, someone steps in and stops it. Members handle things themselves. There is a kind of natural leadership that has emerged within the group.

Many of the members work at the club. Harry Clark, a jovial, heavyset man, is assistant club manager, a trouble-shooter, a kind of man-of-all-work. He works a full week, is paid accordingly, and receives health benefits.

His life was not always like that.

For years it was a succession of fights, hospitalizations, failed marriages, and jobs that led nowhere.

"I hit doctors in the mouth, then patients. I tried to escape from locked wards," he said of his years at Bangor Mental Health Institute, the state hospital for eastern Maine.

"I weighed about two hundred sixty then, and I was hostile. Back then, nobody could tell me what to do."

He drank too much and he took drugs, combining them with medications he was given when released from the hospital. Suicide attempts became his specialty. His nights were spent pacing the floor, obsessing over past details of his life. He did not sleep during the day, either. "During the day, I was thinking of ways to kill myself."

Did he really want to die? "Back then, yes."

He tried gassing himself, standing on the Bangor-Brewer Bridge threatening to jump, and, in the hospital, he tried three times to hang himself with his shoelaces. "The staff had kind of forgotten to take my shoelaces away from me."

Harry can see now that a man who weighed as much as he did could not possibly hang himself with shoelaces. These suicide attempts were based on impulse rather than real planning.

Each time he tried suicide, he was saved, either by the police, the hospital staff, or by neighbors.

The depression that he was finally diagnosed as having began when he was seventeen years old and his grandmother died. She had brought him up, because his alcoholic mother was incapable of taking care of her children.

After the grandmother passed away, "I felt like nobody wanted me.

So I dropped out of school and got a job. I had to support myself. I worked in a woolen mill. I got in fights. I knocked my boss out..." That ended that job.

Then there was a stint in a chicken factory and a half-dozen other menial forms of employment.

Despair pushed him to turn on the gas, but he was rescued by a neighbor in the apartment below and taken to Bangor Mental Health Institute. He would stay there three years, a long time even before the advent of deinstitutionalization. It was in 1973, when treatments were primitive and effective drugs were yet to be developed. Lithium would come along for general use a year later.

Harry immediately underwent six electric shock treatments, without anesthesia, just a hard rubber pacifier in his mouth to keep him from biting his tongue.

Shock treatments were far more cruel then than they are now. In fact, they have made a comeback of sorts, because they do work quickly in alleviating depression. Patients now are given a sedative to ward off the discomfort and the voltage is lower, but the treatments must be done carefully, for they usually cause disorientation and short-term memory loss immediately after being applied.

Most doctors now say that shock was used too much in the 1950's and beyond, before medications became more sophisticated. The treatments were the only way to calm patients, except for insulin shock and baths.

The shock treatments helped Harry to some extent. But his anger and hostility would again turn on the doctors and nurses and he would be given injections that made him sleep for two days or more.

He also was put on one of the early anti-depressants, but it threw him into a manic high, as anti-depressants can do if not monitored, or if the patient has a tendency toward mania.

Of the state hospital, Harry now says, "I don't think I got much help there." When he was released, he was moved to a half-way house, a living arrangement for patients not ready for the community.

Harry immediately saw opportunities to run away from the home, to go from state to state until he was caught and brought back. "I hitched all the way to Florida one time, and supported myself by doing odd jobs. It was great until the State Police found me."

He married his high school sweetheart, a union that lasted three years and was punctuated by drunken fights, beatings and shouting. The marriage produced two children who are grown now and come to see their father every day. They have little memory of the fights because they were so young when their parents divorced.

When he was twenty-three, Harry had to have part of his stomach removed, the result of bleeding ulcers and severe gall bladder disease brought on by heavy drinking. He has been sober ever since and is now thirty-nine years old.

But he has been in and out of the state hospital four times. "It was always the same old routine. I'd try to kill myself and I'd get hauled off to the hospital." There would be more medications, a bit of counseling, a lot of lying around doing nothing."

He began to realize that he became better when he was on the outside instead of the inside. He began going to the Together Place, where he quickly made friends who had been through the same thing as he. "At first I was scared meeting people. The only other friends I'd ever had were drinking friends. You know what I mean?"

The club helped him put things into perspective. No more pacing the floor at night, fewer thoughts of suicide. He married two more times, both marriages failed.

But he is raising an eighteen month old son from the third marriage, something he takes very seriously. "It's wonderful. Someone to love, someone to be responsible for, someone who needs me. I want to be the father I never had," he said.

He never knew his own father, has no idea who he is. "He could be anybody."

He does not have time to think of suicide now, he said. He is too busy with his son, his job and his friends.

The club opens early, around eight o'clock in the morning and stays open for about twelve hours. It is hard to say how many club members there are, for they wander in and out at all hours of the day. The largest crowd is there at noon, to eat. The mentally ill often cannot afford food, even though many of them are on food stamps. So one meal a day at a soup kitchen or a social club can mean a lot. For some who are too sick to cook, it can be the only meal of the day. A number of mentally ill people, especially those who have been hospitalized repeatedly, are afraid of stoves, or do not know how to store food, or shop. There are people who specialize in teaching former patients how to live on their own, how to go to the supermarket, how to fix a frozen dinner. The adjustment to the outside can be more difficult than being in the hospital. There is simply too much stimulation.

Harry has been assistant manager of the Together Place for two years now. He goes to out-patient therapy for depression and is on medication. The last time the illness hit, he was treated by a doctor outside the hospital, treatment that cost hundreds of dollars less than hospitalization, although it is still expensive compared to other medical care.

Maine's social clubs are funded by the state, with federal grants, and through private donations. Often a business or individual will give kitchen equipment, a pool table, or furniture to a club, which usually is part of a larger network of services offered by an agency.

"This place really saved my life," Harry said. "Before, I was working at odd jobs, nothing jobs, and going in and out of the hospital." He believes services for the mentally ill are adequate in Bangor, at least compared with what they used to be. "When I first left the hospital in 1976, there was nothing, no counseling, no social club, no aftercare, no help with housing, no one to care, no nothing," he said. "The only thing I had was being down and out."

Yet he can never be sure he will not be hospitalized again. "I really think I might be. Things are going so good, they're bound to go downhill again, don't you think?"

Our Daughter's Illness is Everything

Robert Treworgy's hands still tremble and his face contorts with grief whenever he tells the story of his daughter and the gun.

"I received a call from the Dean of Students at the University of Maine at Machias. He said, 'Bob, a gun dealer in town just called, and said he sold a gun to Jane. She's left the campus, and we've notified the Sheriff's Department and the State Police,'" the dean said.

Treworgy left his business and rushed home, where he and his wife, Barbara, waited for hours, with thoughts roiling through their heads of their youngest child taking her own life on one of the many back roads leading to Calais at the tip of Washington County.

The gun dealer had thought better of his sale after observing the young woman's behavior and had called the school.

Jane Treworgy did not kill herself, instead, she returned home where her horrified father removed the gun from the trunk of her car. "I had never even handled a gun before. And it was a great big gun, with a box of shells," he said.

Bob Treworgy is a man of slight build, with a gentle manner, and a kind face. He is a retired pharmacist who owned three drugstores in the Calais area. Barbara is more outgoing than her husband, with a direct manner of speech and a jolly sense of humor.

The gun episode happened more than fifteen years ago, after two years of escalating behavior that convinced Bob and Barbara that something was terribly wrong.

Jane's signs of mental illness began innocently enough, just as they do with many people. She spent two years at Gould Academy in Bethel, then asked if she could finish her education at Calais High School.

There, she was head cheerleader and popular with her classmates. It was during her years at Westbrook College that she called home and asked if her parents would mind if she saw a psychiatrist.

"I said, 'certainly,'" her mother remembers. "It was kind of the in thing to see a psychiatrist then. I didn't think anything about it."

But the summer after Jane graduated from Westbrook with a two-year degree, her parents began to suspect something was wrong. She was working on the coast, and whenever her parents visited and took her to the theatre or to other summer activities, she was incapable of concentrating.

"She'd jump up and leave, and go call her psychiatrist," her father said. "She'd jump up and down, and up and down. We knew that wasn't normal."

He remembers getting tickets to a Frank Sinatra concert, something that meant a great deal to Bob and Barbara. During the concert, Jane repeatedly left to call her doctor's office. "I followed her out at one point, and I said, 'Honey, this concert is pretty important. I went to all the trouble of getting tickets. Don't you think you could come back and try to enjoy it?"

Jane, meanwhile, decided to take a third year of college at the University of Maine at Farmington. There, she began falling apart. She started a cheering club and became completely obsessed with it, and with what she perceived as a lack of effort and school spirit by the other girls.

By the following summer, she was living at home and Barbara was driving her to Bangor twice a week for therapy, a two hundred mile round trip. There were not, and are not, any psychiatric services in Washington County. No crisis beds, no full time psychiatrist, no hotline, nowhere to go for acute care except the hospital emergency room where patients wait hours to be transported to Bangor.

Even the Treworgy's neighbor, a family physician, pooh-poohed Jane's behavior by saying it was a phase that many young people go through and that she would snap out of it. The Treworgy's friends took much the same attitude.

It was not long before the scenes inside the house began. Some nights Jane would decide at ten o'clock that she wanted to go out to the family's camp. Sometimes she went, other times the parents were able to calm her down with a sleeping pill or by talking to her. "I would hug her and say, 'You don't want to go out there tonight, dear. It's too cold out there, uncomfortable,'" Bob said.

"By this time, we knew she was not right," he said. Barbara found a razor blade in Jane's coat pocket, and the girl at other times flew into unexpected fits of rage. One time, her mother said, she flung a large pot of creamed corn from the stove to the ceiling, splattering it everywhere. She then kicked in the doors of a small hutch cupboard in the kitchen.

She was admitted to the psychiatric unit at Eastern Maine Medical Center in Bangor, where she checked herself out after two days. She came home and almost immediately took an overdose of sleeping pills, not enough to harm herself, but enough to convince her parents that she was desperately in need of more help. "We just thought that our world was falling apart," Barbara said. "What was happening to our little girl?"

Jane is the youngest of four children. A family portrait shows her smiling, a petite girl with dark hair. "To look at her, you'd never know she had mental illness," her father said gently.

By almost any standards, especially in Washington County, the family would be considered well-off financially. Bob sold his drugstores. The family received an inheritance from a relative and were able to afford private high school and expensive colleges for all four children. One son is a pharmacist, another is a psychiatrist.

"But we have spent more on Jane than on educating the other three put together," Bob said. "We could have educated her four or five times over for what we've spent," he said.

Jane long ago used up the twenty-five thousand dollar lifetime cap that insurance companies allowed for mental illness at the time she became sick. The Maine Legislature this year lifted that cap and made coverage of mental illness comparable to that of other illnesses. The law is too late for Jane.

Her expenses have been borne primarily by her family, although she does receive some disability. Her parents do not want her to go on food stamps and other entitlements.

Jane's first long hospitalization came at St. Mary's Hospital in Lewiston after the gun incident. Bob heard of the hospital from a friend, after the one in Bangor was reluctant to take Jane again because she had not stayed for treatment previously.

"Two-thirds of the way across the state. Strange doctors, a strange hospital," Bob said of St. Mary's. When he walked into the psychiatric unit, it was just like a scene from *One Flew Over the Cuckoo's Nest*," he said. At that time, adolescents and adults were on the same unit. Bob and Barbara's first encounter was with a drooling woman wearing a large feather boa who kept grabbing at Bob, pulling on his hands and his pant leg.

"Then she took this boy about fourteen years old who was tall for his age, and the two of them walked up and down the hall together, up and down, up and down." Bob was not sure if he wanted to leave his daughter there or not.

That was more than ten years ago, and the hospital now has separate units for adolescents and adults, structured programs and outpatient services with excellent reputations.

Jane was helped there, by a fine doctor who has since retired. Bob and Barbara settled into a routine. Each Friday afternoon, they would leave Calais, drive to Lewiston, and take a room near the hospital.

"Some nights we'd drive back from Lewiston and it would be snowing, so we'd spend the night in Bangor. We would be so exhausted, and Jane would have seemed worse to us than she had the weekend before. We'd get to our room and just hug and cry and say, 'What are we going to do?'" Bob said.

He weeps as he recalls the Christmas that Jane was at St. Mary's. Usually Christmas would be spent in the large Treworgy home on the outskirts of Calais, the home with the gingerbread trim, with brocade furniture, antiques and beautiful dishes for the Christmas meal.

That year, "We took a suite at the Holiday Inn in Auburn. I took down a little tree with all the presents. We set up a Christmas in that room. I was allowed to take Jane out for that one day, and our other three kids all came and spent Christmas with us. They did that for their sister," Bob said with tears in his eyes.

"He becomes very upset over all this," Barbara says by way of explanation. "He often breaks down."

"I've cursed God," Bob continued. "When this first happened, I would get on my knees and ask God to take me, anything, as long as she could get well."

"It is God-awful," he said. "I'm a pharmacist. I have financial resources. What about the people who go through this who don't have what we have?"

In those cases, families have to turn to the state to put their children on disability, food stamps, Medicaid. That usually happens when the insurance runs out, which does not take long if there is a lengthy hospitalization. For those with no insurance, the access to psychiatric services can be very difficult, if not impossible, depending upon where people live. If they live in rural Maine, a child can go untreated. If they live from Augusta or Portland, there are doctors, sliding-fee clinics, group homes and a number of doctors who take Medicaid. But, some do not.

Meanwhile, parents of mentally ill young people often begin to think everything will be all right if their child just marries the right person. At one point, the Treworgys thought Jane was going to marry a doctor and their hopes soared. He was a medical student at the University of Vermont, where Jane's brother was a student. Jane was a patient at the clinic there.

She went to the clinic after coming home from St. Mary's with a contract for living at home, then breaking it within two weeks by stealing pills from her father's drugstore.

By this time, she had been tested and analyzed and diagnosed as obsessive-compulsive with borderline personality disorder.

"Borderline personality disorder, that doesn't sound so bad," Barbara said with a laugh. It is amusing until one reads what people with that disorder do, she said.

Borderline personality disorder was a common diagnosis at one time, but is rarely used as a primary diagnosis today. Victims of it are likely to cut or mutilate themselves, exercise poor judgement and impulse control, and be subject to mood swings. Today the diagnosis is more likely to be bipolar illness or affective disorder which is treated with medication, especially lithium.

On the way to Vermont, the Treworgys had to spend the night. Jane had her own room, and in the middle of the night, she flew from her room and began pounding on her parents' door, screaming that they were putting her away, that she would not go. The other guests were awakened by the commotion, and Bob and Barbara were forced to pull her inside to calm her down.

She spent several months at the Vermont Medical Center, was tested and re-tested and found to have schizo-affective disorder, a tough illness characterized by features of schizophrenia and manic-depression. "They said something in her brain hadn't developed properly," her father said.

The mixture of the two illnesses, one a thought disorder, the other a mood disorder, carries with it paranoia, delusions, depression, mania, fantasies, inability to cope with the outside world, and breaks with reality.

"The medical center kept her for months, then put her in a group home, where she received therapy every blessed day," Barbara said.

Meanwhile, she dated the young doctor for six years, even going to Chicago with him for three years while he completed his residency. Bob remembers feeling, "We've been blessed. This doctor is going to marry Jane, and everything is going to be all right." The doctor was convinced he could make Jane's life serene, just by catering to her. He did not seem to see the seriousness of her illness.

"It was the strongest case of blind love that I've ever seen," Bob said.

Instead of marrying him, Jane moved out on him, saying she loved him only as a friend.

She is now thirty-eight, has been hospitalized eight times, all for extended periods, and lives in Bangor where she has her own apartment and sees a doctor at Acadia Hospital every week.

Her parents, meanwhile, have sold their stock and a piece of property to pay for her care. They have also dipped heavily into savings. Both say they would give up everything except their home and Social Security if Jane could become well.

"There are such feelings of sadness and frustration and wishing we could find the answer," Bob said. There is also a feeling of isolation from friends who mean well, but really do not understand. "They keep saying that Jane can snap out of it," Barbara said.

Bob is frustrated that no medication does the trick. Jane was on Resperadone, the latest medication for schizo-affective disorders, but doctors then insisted on trying Clozaril. The side effect of excessive drooling was dreadful, her parents said. At night she was soaking her nightgown, her pillow, her sheets. She tried putting towels over her pillows, but in the morning everything would still be drenched. Her quality of life was nil, her father said. She has since gone back to the other medication.

Bob pays for Jane's apartment, with the exception of a small amount that she pays from her disability check. Her check would not stretch far enough for a decent rent, her mother said. The parents. who go to Bangor every week and stay at least one night, say it is just as cheap in the long run to have a place in Bangor as it is to pay for meals and hotel rooms.

"She isn't well enough to cope," Barbara said of the frequency of the visits. Jane can not drive anymore, she lives in a constant state of paranoia, and she has no friends. She calls home at least once a day, usually more.

"We spend two or three days in Bangor," Barbara said. "We get her out, we help her with the laundry, Bob does the grocery shopping, or washes the windows, or makes small repairs around the apartment."

Usually there is some kind of crisis. Jane, at one point, became obsessed with the thought that someone would come in and steal her cat. Bob had to ask the landlord to put a bolt lock on the inside of the door to calm Jane's fears.

Bob and Barbara are very active in the Alliance for the Mentally Ill of Maine and have started a local chapter in Washington County, where people are reluctant to admit a family member's illness to the outside world. The attitude is, "This is our problem. We'll deal with it ourselves."

While the material from the Alliance tells family members to develop their own interests and not dwell on the mental illness, Barbara says Jane is her only interest.

"Our daughter's illness is everything. If she's having a bad day, we have a bad day. If she's having a good day, we have a good day. This is my life now, as long as I'm on this earth," she said.

"She's as well as she's ever going to be. This is the way it is, and I've come to accept that," she said.

Some People Have No Sympathy

After Doris Dudly finished playing some country and western songs on the piano, she asked for a ride to K-Mart. She was planning a little shopping, then supper at Wendy's.

"I won't be here for dinner, Florence," she told the matron at the elegant retirement home where Doris lives.

Doris is eighty-three years old, yet in some way has just started to live within the past ten years.

She had an unhappy marriage, and earlier, a domineering mother who caused unimaginable trouble within the family, Doris said.

And for twenty years, Doris suffered from an illness that just recently has gained attention within the medical community: Depression among the elderly.

Doris was so sick that many of those twenty years of depression that started when she was fifty were spent in bed weeping and moaning. There were stays at hospital, electric shock therapy, Valium and other tranquilizers, and the feeling on her part that she was going to stay depressed forever.

After her husband died, she hired a housekeeper, then dismissed her. "I thought I could take care of myself."

She could not.

"I laid in bed all day and cried. And when I ate, I'd take a can of beans or corned beef hash, put it in the oven for a few minutes, then eat it right out of the can. That's how much strength and interest I had in things."

She rarely bathed, seldom changed her clothes, and would sleep in the same clothes she had worn for days.

"When I came here, I was a mess," she said of coming to the retirement home ten years ago. She had just been released from the psychiatric unit at Kennebec Valley Medical Center, and had been told she had to go to a home to live, a place where she could be supervised and have other people around.

"Every place we went to, my daughter wouldn't leave me there. They weren't fit to live in," she said of Augusta's choice of housing for the mentally ill. Her daughter, a social worker, talked to the people at the retirement home and Doris was accepted.

"I don't know why they ever took me," she said. "I can't help but think it had something to do with the fact that I had the money."

The home promotes gracious living and is designed for older women who can pay for their board and room at a fairly high rate. In return, the women are given excellent care, beautiful meals and a chance to retain their dignity. All who live there must be in general good health, able to come to the table for meals and independent enough to take care of themselves.

Doris wasn't any of those things when she first arrived. "I just laid in bed and cried," she said. "I couldn't read the newspaper, because I couldn't concentrate. I was very confused. I couldn't hold a thought. I'd think of something, then immediately forget it. And I didn't mingle with the other women, for fear I'd say something that didn't make sense."

When she left the hospital, she was given a new antidepressant, a kind of last attempt to make her better. Within six weeks, the pills began to work. "I first found that I could read the paper. Then I wasn't having so many crying jags. It's not like I felt better all at once after six weeks, it was more gradual. Then I decided I'd like to play the piano again, so I began practicing an hour a day. That really helped me get better."

These days she wakes up early, after going to bed late, and thinks about all the things she wants to do that day. There is hand-sewing for herself and the other residents. She makes braided rugs. The library is right across the street.

"Sometimes I get antsy in here," she said of living in one room, despite its fine furnishings. "These ladies here, I love them dearly, but they live in the past."

She also plays bridge daily, never missing a game.

Doris thinks depression in the elderly is simply sloughed off, chalked up to old age. And it often is. The signs of hostility, sadness, loss of appetite, and confusion sometimes are ignored as just part of the aging process. But with the proper medication, older people can remain free from such symptoms.

The elderly suffer a great many losses: Spouses, sometimes homes, the loss of vitality and robust health, and the loss of children who have grown up and left home. Depression can set in, especially if the person is moved to a nursing home or even a retirement center.

"You have to go through it before you can appreciate it," Doris said of her illness. "So many people have no sympathy."

"I spoke up at the table one day," she continued. "There was a woman here that I knew was going through exactly what I went through, and the other residents were grumbling about why she needed a tray brought to her room and all that. And I told them, you have to experience depression to know how bad it really is. It takes everything out of you, mentally and physically. So I told them to be more sympathetic to that woman. And afterward, some of the women thanked me for bringing that out."

"There's a stigma around this and other mental illnesses, and there always will be. Sometimes I'd meet someone, and I'd start twittering, and they'd say, 'Oh, she's the one who had the problems…you know.'"

Doris grew up in Bangor in what she calls a normal family that had what it needed, but no extra money.

"But I'll tell you one thing. I had a very domineering mother, and she lived to be ninety-two. You can't imagine the trouble she caused in our family, subtle things. I loved her, because she was my mother, but I never liked her."

As an example, Doris's only sister became pregnant before she was married, something to be ashamed of years ago. "And instead of putting her arms around my sister and telling her it would turn out all right, my mother never forgave her," Doris said. "When we were older, we found out that our mother had done the same thing herself. She had had to get married."

Doris went to work after high school, then met Charlie Dudley. Their courtship lasted nine years, and she was twenty-eight when they married.

"He never loved me," she said. "That's why it took us so long to marry. I just kept hanging on. I loved him. And I think there was some pressure from his family for him to marry me," she said.

The marriage was wrong from the start, she said, despite its lasting forty years. Charlie was a cold man, a distant fellow who never complimented his wife or showed her any affection. He was quiet, antisocial and thought it was the man's place to handle financial affairs and have the last word on everything, his wife said.

"It was the biggest mistake of my life," she said of the marriage. He was never mean to her physically, he provided well for the family, and he gave his three children the best educations possible.

But there was never a "You did a good job," or "I'm proud of you," or "That was a good meal. Can I help with the dishes?"

Charlie was an auditor who really wanted to be a farmer, his wife said. And when he died, he left her very well off. "I never even have to think about money. And everytime I go on a shopping spree today, I say, 'Thank you, Charlie.'"

"We had no communication," she said. "That was the problem. If I said anything, he'd make out like I didn't know what I was talking about. So it was always small talk, what the kids were doing and that kind of thing. We didn't know how to have a good fight."

"I'll tell you something. Communication is the most important thing in a marriage. It's more important than sex. It's more important than love, even," she said.

The couple lived all over the country, until Charlie retired at the age of fifty-five after coming into some money. At that point, he began to drink heavily. "He'd start around noon, and by night, he was pretty well tanked. And he was a loner. He didn't want anyone around. I remember when our daughter took piano lessons, and, of course, she had to practice. Well, her practicing bothered him so much in the afternoon when he was drinking that we had to move the piano up into her bedroom."

Doris, the outgoing member of the couple, threw herself into outside activities to dull the pain of rejection. She was in civic groups, church activities, women's clubs. "I think everyone knew what our marriage was like. And I think Charlie was jealous of my outgoing personality."

Her depression began when her husband retired and began drinking. "It started with crying jags. I told myself I wasn't going for any help, so I toughed it out."

She had children to care for, meals to fix and a house to take care of, all when the only thing she wanted to do was crawl into bed and sleep.

"I finally wound up going to five psychiatrists," she said, after a church counselor recommended it. "Charlie willingly paid for them. And I was in and out of four hospitals, for as long as four months at a time. I had shock treatment, they put me on Valium and just about everything else they had back then. But they didn't have the medications then."

Charlie paid the hospital bills, thousands of dollars worth, without complaint. And at that time, there was no insurance coverage for mental illness treatment. His bills must have run close to a quarter of a million dollars.

Doctors said her depression was a combination of heredity and the years of rejection from her husband. Doris's grandmother and sister both had what were called "nervous breakdowns" and a son later developed a depressive disorder.

Even when he was dying, Doris's husband did not want her near him, she said. "He just asked for some cold water. He didn't want anything from me. So he died alone, in that bed, all by himself."

She thinks her husband rejected her because she always had weight problems. "He never liked heavy people, and I was always heavy. I even went to Duke University at one point and lost sixty pounds to try to please him. But I gained it all back, of course. And it didn't make any difference."

In Maine, Doris was treated at Seton Hospital in Waterville, at Eastern Maine Medical Center in Bangor, and finally, at Kennebec Valley Medical Center, where she was put on the drug that did the trick.

"Some of these hospitals do something that I don't like," she said. "They have a structure and a scheduled program, and you have to take part in it, no matter how awful you feel. I'd do what I had to do for their program, then I'd crawl into bed," she said.

The most common feature of depression is extreme fatigue. The patient often sleeps as much as twenty hours a day, yet still does not feel rested. For most, there is a certain time of day when the darkness disappears and the person can feel quite normal. For Doris, it was evening. "I've always been a night person. I don't go to sleep now until around one a.m."

There was a time, she said, when her family and the doctors simply gave up on her. She was told by people to "snap out of it," she was put on treatment after treatment, and she put her family through hell, she said.

When her son went through his depression, he said to his mother, "You know, I used to get so disgusted with you when you were depressed, but now I know what it's like, and I would never think that way again."

After she became a widow, Doris hired the housekeeper, because she was thought to be incapable of caring for herself. When the housekeeper left, Doris went right downhill, with more crying, poor hygiene and malnutrition.

"Mornings were hell. Sometimes I did't get up until two o'clock in the afternoon."

Where she lives now, she must dress for the day before coming down to the breakfast table, something she resented at first, but now thinks is a good thing. "A lot of these women, like me, would like to wear a bathrobe to breakfast. But if you do that, you're likely to scuff around half the day in your housecoat," she said.

Doris is a careful dresser. Her earrings match her necklace, which in turn matches her bracelets. "Everything has to be coordinated," she said of herself. "And my daughters are the same way."

Both her daughters, she said, married domineering men, and both divorced. "I couldn't do that. I didn't have any money of my own. I didn't have anything to fall back on. I had to ask Charlie for every bit of money I had, and that's not good in a marriage. He'd always say things like, 'What happened to that five dollars I gave you the other day?'"

Doris never thought of suicide, but when her son was sick, the family worried that he might take his own life. "My God, he was full of rage, and it was all directed at his father. We really thought he might kill himself."

While the son had enough energy to show rage, Doris's depressions were such that she was rendered helpless. "I couldn't do anything."

People as depressed as that rarely take their own lives, because they simply do not have the energy to carry out such an act.

When she was hospitalized, Doris saw a number of elderly people being treated for depression. Yet only in the past four or five years has any attention been paid to the problem. There are studies showing that most suicides are men who kill themselves after retirement age, or when they begin to go downhill physically.

Doris sees a psychiatrist every six months, at an office right across the way from the retirement home. "And I can call her day or night, if I need to see her more frequently."

She takes two antidepressants a day to stay on an even keel. "I still have days when I don't have much motivation, but I think that's my age. I just know that I look forward to something each day."

I Missed Everything

Eddie Handy's first job was not pumping gas or mowing lawns. It was putting hard rubber stoppers into the mouths of patients brought in for electric shock treatments at the Augusta Mental Health Institute.

Handy was twelve years old, just a boy. He was not really a patient at the hospital, he was incarcerated there for running away from reform school after being beaten too many times.

He was to stay at Augusta Mental Health Institute for twenty-six years, until 1976, when laws changed and he was released along with hundreds of other patients who had been there too long, many for all the wrong reasons.

"There was one guy who was there fifty years for stealing chickens. He came there in the 1920's, and the hospital lost all his records over the years," Handy said.

Handy lives in Portland now. He looks a little like the comedian and musician Steve Allen. He has total recall of his years at the state hospital.

"There were twenty beds lined up in the day room," he said of the section where shock treatment was given. The patient would be brought in, strapped down, and Handy would insert the rubber tube. Electricity would surge through the brain, sending the patient into convulsions before sleep took over.

"Imagine, twelve, thirteen years old, standing there doing that," Handy, fifty-seven, says today.

He was sent to reform school for setting small fires in graveyards when he was a kid. He and friends used to do it for kicks until a friend snitched on him to police.

Handy was sent to a boys's school, where he was struck by older kids too many times and began running away.

"So one night, the head of the school said, 'Want to take a ride, Eddie?' And the next thing I knew, we were at the state hospital," he said. "There were no young kids there then, just rapists and killers, some from the state prison. Lifers, you know."

"There were fights every two minutes, and the place was full of old men, always arguing, arguing about the food, about whether they could have seconds. There were no seconds in those days," he said.

It soon became apparent in listening to Handy that one of the ways he survived was through humor. He can make a funny story out what must have been the most frightening and bleak conditions.

"Jesus, the food was terrible," he said, a topic he referred to several times. He also asks people over and over if they knew former patients and doctors from the hospital. The questions can be annoying until one considers that Augusta Mental Health Institute was Handy's home for twenty-six years, his neighborhood, a small town where the population reached two thousand two hundred men and women during his stay.

"The unit I was in first had eighty men on it, it should have had about sixty. And there were no drugs then, no drugs at all. There was nothing to calm people down except shock treatment. Or, once in a while, they'd give you an insulin shot in the ass. I don't know what that was supposed to do," he said.

"I had to wait thirty years for a diagnosis," he said. The hospital simply listed him as a wild kid. No diagnosis, no attempt at one.

In the meantime, an older patient who had killed his wife took Handy under his wing and refused to let the other patients bother the boy. "He wouldn't let anyone come near me. He had killed his wife, but he was a good man to me," he said.

In return for protection, Handy made the old man's bed and did other little things for him.

"As I said, the food was terrible," he said, returning to his favorite topic. "Everything was all mashed up, you know? We had beans all the time, it seemed. Meat about once a week. The only thing I ate was macaroni and cheese on Thursday nights. Thursday was macaroni and cheese day," he said.

During those years, people were put into Augusta Mental Health Institute and forgotten. The assumption was that they would be there for good, and the place was used both for mental treatment and as a place to be punished. The state paid little heed to the hospital or its budget, although the hospital is right across the street from the State House, in plain view of lawmakers.

Handy remembers one female patient who underwent nine shock treatments while pregnant. "It killed her baby," he said. Labor was induced so she could deliver a dead child.

Handy moved on to other jobs as he became older, primarily making beds and washing floors. "And I took care of old men's dirty laundry for twenty years. Now, if you don't think that was something," he said.

He said the aides on duty during the day used to lie about the behavior of the patients to the night crew, so that certain patients would be punished. Once drugs came along, the punishment was extra shots of Thorazine. Before that, it might be maximum security for a period of weeks or months.

"I was in maximum security once because I broke a window. Other times, I fought with the staff," he said.

Handy said he was never beaten or truly abused, but he was thrown down on a hard floor once.

"It was at night and I was taking a leak, and this aide said, 'Handy, get to bed right now.' I said, 'Give me some room to breathe, will ya?' And he grabbed me around the neck from behind. I didn't see him coming. He flung me right down on the floor, one of those cement bathroom floors," he said.

Handy is silent for several seconds. Then, "I saw three employees kill a patient. They'll tell you today that it never happened, but it did, I saw it. I was lying near a vent. It was a cold night and I was trying to keep warm.

"This patient did something and three staffers jumped him and choked him to death. They hushed that right up," he said of the former hospital administration.

When the State Police came, all the patients were herded into a dining room. Police were told that the man had hanged himself or suffocated or something.

"They called his wife to tell her about it, and she said she didn't want the body, so he was buried in a pauper's grave somewhere," he said.

Handy was barely a teenager when he witnessed the murder. Years later, in 1988, he was at the hospital for another stay when five patients died during a heat wave. "That wasn't all the fault of the heat, you know. The medications the patients were on were too high for that kind of weather. They kept trying to get the doctor to lower the dosages, but he wouldn't. So it was partly that doctor's fault," he said.

While other teens in the 1950's were going to the beach, listening to popular music and dancing with friends, Handy had only a small radio, his only contact with the reality of what other kids his age were doing.

And he loved the show "American Bandstand." Others would want to watch the baseball games during the afternoons, but Handy stood his ground. "I'd protect that TV set for hours, so I could watch that show," he said.

He had no other normal growing up experiences. He apparently never had a girlfriend, much less a wife and children. He never learned to drive, and now depends upon city transportation or his mother for rides. His mother is seventy-seven and brings his supper over to him every night.

"I never learned how to cook," he said. "I live mostly on orange juice. I don't eat very well." He has his own apartment as part of Shalom House, Inc., which provides low-rent housing for the mentally ill.

"I have a living room, a bedroom, a bathroom and a kitchen. But the girls here, they're all psychotic. I don't like that kind of girl," he said.

He tries to make friends, with moderate success. Recently he bought a female neighbor a rose, which she seemed to appreciate. She and her boyfriend were having a cookout and Handy felt they should have offered him a hamburger. "It would have been the polite thing to do," he said. "What would be so hard about saying, 'Have a hamburger'?" He was hurt by the perceived rejection.

At Augusta Mental Health Institute, that kind of thing did not happen, said Handy, who admitted he became attached to patients "like you would an uncle or a brother."

When he returned to the hospital in 1988, he found more cruelty than he had seen in the previous twenty-six years that he was there. "They were meaner to the women patients," he said of female staff.

He told a story of a staffer taking a patient out for a cigarette break.

The patient either said something or was not smoking fast enough to please the staffer. "And she said to this patient, 'No more cigarette breaks for you today.' Then she cuffed this patient in the side of the head, you know. Cuffed her. There was no need of that," he said.

When he was at Augusta Mental Health Institute originally, staff and patients formed a kind of bond. The staff knew the patients well. The patients were not expected to leave anytime soon, and as long as patients did not make too much trouble, things went along quite smoothly.

But by 1988, the hospital was in crisis. There had been more than a decade of releasing patients into the community and Maine's cities were overflowing with former patients who had no outside services or support.

The hospital was blamed. It was also blamed for its treatment of patients, for by this time, the plight of the mentally ill had become an issue and advocates were springing up to protect and expand patients' rights. The hospital also lost its accreditation, because of the staffing shortages and sloppy record keeping, among other violations. Medicaid money was withheld until a sincere effort was made to improve conditions.

Unflattering publicity and legislative inquiry led to the AMHI consent decree, an agreement between the state and patients who sued over the lack of services and the inhumane conditions at the hospital. The state is still working toward the 1997 compliance date for the decree.

Handy, meanwhile, kept up with current events while he squandered twenty-six years at Augusta Mental Health Institute. He remembers the death of John Kennedy, the first moon shot and other historic milestones. But life generally revolved around the institution.

"I wasn't allowed to go to downtown Augusta until the 1970's," he said. The first time he went, he walked just outside the yellow line at a cross walk, and a cop hollered, "If I catch you doing that again, you bastard, I'll put you in jail," Handy recalls.

"Bully boys, you know," he said of the Augusta police.

He did get to dance with women from time to time, at hospital socials. The men who were not too old would go into the women's section and dance. But there was no girl for Handy. He learned about sex and took care of his sexual urges by reading erotic magazines that a friend used to buy for him.

Once in a while a woman would come into the men's ward wearing a nightgown with nothing under it. She would pull up the gown and ask if anyone felt like making love, Handy said. He would take her arm and gently lead her back to her own ward.

But there was one staffer who arranged to have prostitutes from Portland visit the hospital. "He had a little room next to where he worked," Handy said. "The girls were often invited up on weekends. The patients never got to do anything with them, just the staff. I was called to the police station to see if I could identify any of the girls through pictures, and I did. There was this one girl with a tattoo on her leg. I received eleven dollars for my information. The staffer was fired. And the hospital hushed the whole thing up again," he said.

The advent of Thorazine changed not only Augusta Mental Health Institute, but all of mental health. The use of it and its later spin-offs enabled hospitals to release patients into the community as long as they stayed on the medication. The drug, a powerful sedative, also could be used to calm patients when nothing else had helped.

Handy remembers the exact year that Augusta Mental Health Institute began using it, 1959. "They put everyone on Thorazine," he said. "We used to have these wooden benches all around the ward, and they had to get pillows because patients were lying down all the time."

"It makes you drowsy and weak, you know. And then the nurse would say, 'Why is Handy lying down? Put him to work.'" So Handy would mop his floors and do the laundry in a stupor.

Thorazine also was used as a weapon. If someone misbehaved, give him a shot. If someone got out of bed at night, give him an extra dose of Thorazine.

There was a time when Handy's father also was at Augusta Mental Health Institute, at the same time as his son. Handy does not like to talk about that. "My father was not mentally ill. He might have been disturbed. When he got mad, though, it would take twelve to thirteen men to handle him," he said.

Handy recalled one night when his father was sewing a button on his one shirt after patients were supposed to be in bed. An aide walked by and said, "What are you doing out of bed?" The father said he was just fixing his shirt. A doctor going through the ward said, "Give him another shot of Thorazine."

Patients were not supposed to leave their beds at night, except to go to the bathroom, and the lights went out fairly early, by ten o'clock.

When visitors came to see the patients, they were allowed to stay one hour. Handy's parents usually came up from Portland once a month to see their son. He always asked them to bring four or five Italian sandwiches, as they were called in Maine then, because the food at the hospital was so bland. He would share the sandwiches with other patients.

"When I got out of the hospital, I could not get enough cheeseburgers, hamburgers, pizza pies, Dagwoods, all that kind of thing," he said. "I love those fast food places."

Handy is quite sure he was one of two of the youngest patients ever sent to Augusta Mental Health Institute before the hospital opened an adolescent unity.

"I was there, and Jesus, they later had this seven-year-old kid in maximum security. He'd killed another child. They used to bring funny books into him," he said.

At that time, Maine had no correctional facilities for children that young and it still does not. The age for sending young people to the Maine Youth Center is twelve. The only alternative is out-of-state incarceration, or sending the child to one of the two private psychiatric hospitals in Maine that treat children. One hospital is in Bangor, the other, Portland.

Handy says two things got him out of Augusta Mental Health Institute. "My doctor died and the laws changed. Otherwise, I'd still be there," he said. He claims not to be bitter about his experience. "I blame the doctors, I don't blame the hospital. It's the doctors who kept me there. And besides, it's all in the past now," he said.

When he was released, he lived in a series of boarding homes. One was in Monmouth, where the farm family used to take the bulk of his disability check and give him a small allowance. "They'd hide the money down by the pig sty," he said.

He moved to a rooming house in Augusta where the owner did the same thing, giving Handy forty-five dollars a month and keeping nearly four hundred dollars for room and board. He also lived in Belgrade briefly, where the food was terrible, he said.

Then he moved in with his mother in Portland in 1981. "There was nothing in Portland, nothing for the mentally ill then," he said of housing and services. In 1988, he threatened his mother and was sent back to the hospital for a year. Then he was diagnosed as manic depressive. "That's not as bad as schizophrenia, is it?" he asked, anxiously.

He admitted he becomes agitated and flies off the handle, yet he takes medication and insists he's mostly just excitable. He has a case worker, but if he feels a real crisis coming on, he calls his mother.

"I missed everything," he says of his years at the hospital when he is pressed on the question. "And I've only got a few years left now. The Thorazine and Lithium have affected my kidneys. I've got two cats. That's all I have."